JOHN PIPER

ASTONISHED BY GOD

TEN TRUTHS TO TURN *the* WORLD UPSIDE DOWN

Astonished by God: Ten Truths to Turn the World Upside Down

(This book originally appeared under the title *Doctrine Matters*.)

Copyright © 2018 by Desiring God
Post Office Box 2901
Minneapolis, MN 55402

Published for Desiring God by

CruciformPress

Print/PDF 978-1-941114-55-1
Mobipocket 978-1-941114-56-8
ePub 978-1-941114-57-5

Unless otherwise indicated,
Scripture quotations are from the ESV Bible
(*The Holy Bible, English Standard* © 2001 by Crossway).
Scripture quotations marked NAS or NASB are taken from the New American Standard Bible® (NASB), Copyright © 1960, 1962, 1963, 1968, 1971, 1972, 1973, 1975, 1977, 1995 by The Lockman Foundation.
Used by permission.

All emphases in Scripture quotations have been added by the author.

Contents

Author

John Piper is a founder of desiringGod.org, and chancellor of Bethlehem College & Seminary in Minneapolis, Minnesota. He served for thirty-three years as pastor of Bethlehem Baptist Church and is author of more than fifty books. More than thirty years of his sermons and articles are available at desiringGod.org.

Preface

I wonder if you associate the words *astonishment* and *compassion* with the word *doctrine*? I do. And not only those words, but also *joy* and *life* and *hope*.

Doctrine simply means "teaching." It has come to refer to groups of teachings, usually held by a religious group, but every place *doctrine* occurs in the Bible it simply translates the ordinary word for teaching.

So, when Jesus saw the crowds who were "like sheep without a shepherd," Mark tells us that he had compassion on them and "began to teach them many things" (Mark 6:34). Jesus's compassion elicits teaching—doctrine.

This is what Jesus did more than anything else: he taught. "Jesus went throughout all the cities and villages, teaching" (Matthew 9:35). And usually the response was astonishment. "When the crowd heard it, they were astonished at his teaching" (Matthew 22:33). Astonishment is elicited by Jesus's teaching—doctrine.

It is simply amazing the way the apostle John connects doctrine with our relationship to God. He says, "Everyone who does not abide in the *doctrine* of Christ, *does not have God*. Whoever abides in the *doctrine* has both the Father and the Son" (2 John 1:9). If we tenaciously treasure true teaching from Jesus, we have God. Amazing.

Not surprisingly, then, Jesus tells us that his teaching is for our "joy" (John 15:11) and our "life" (John 6:68). And the apostle Paul said that all the doctrine of the Bible is for our "hope" (Romans 15:4).

So, when I was coming to the end of my 33 years as pastor at Bethlehem Baptist Church in Minneapolis, Minnesota, it seemed good to look back over the decades and distill the doctrines—the astonishing, compassionate, life-giving, joy-awakening, hope-sustaining teachings— that held everything together.

That is what I did in my final sermons at the church. I think of them as legacy messages. What were the main truths I wanted to leave ringing in my peoples' ears? I ended up with ten of them, ten truths that have turned my world upside down, and turned our church upside down, and will continue to turn the whole world upside down as the gospel advances by the power of God. In this book, I want to walk you through those ten truths, much as I did in those final sermons at Bethlehem. Indeed, this book is a summary of the main things I tried to impart during those 33 years.

But it would be a mistake to read this book in a nostalgic mood. These messages are future-oriented. They are for living life today and tomorrow. I explain in chapter one that the aim was not to *land* the plane after a 33-year flight at Bethlehem, but to *launch* two new seasons of life—

theirs and mine. Because these doctrines are, as you will soon read, "wildly untamable, explosively uncontainable, and electrically future-creating."

Every day is the launch of the rest of your life. You are not bound by your past. Not if you turn to Jesus and believe his teaching. Not if you are astonished by God. Instead, you will know the truth—the doctrine—and the truth will set you free (John 8:32).

John Piper
Minneapolis, Minnesota
March 2018

EXODUS 3:13-15

Then Moses said to God, "If I come to the people of Israel and say to them, 'The God of your fathers has sent me to you,' and they ask me, 'What is his name?' what shall I say to them?" [14] God said to Moses, "I AM WHO I AM." And he said, "Say this to the people of Israel: 'I AM has sent me to you.'" [15] God also said to Moses, "Say this to the people of Israel: 'The LORD, the God of your fathers, the God of Abraham, the God of Isaac, and the God of Jacob, has sent me to you.' This is my name forever, and thus I am to be remembered throughout all generations."

1
God Is

My ultimate goal in the ten chapters of this book is to spread a passion for the supremacy of God in all things for the joy of all peoples through Jesus Christ. In other words, I aim to make so much of God the Father, and God the Son, through God the Spirit, that you will be moved to join me in glad adoration of our triune God.

Under that overarching aim, my goal is to awaken and strengthen a powerful conviction in you as you read. When I delivered these messages to Bethlehem Baptist Church at the conclusion of my 33 years of ministry there, I wanted the people to see them as preparation, not consummation. Or to put it another way, I hoped to help them see and feel that my transition away from being pastor was, for the church and for me, less about landing and more about launching. It was less about the great things God *had* done, and more about the greater things God is going to do.

Therefore it seemed good to me, with the encouragement of Bethlehem's pastoral staff, to turn the church's attention to a battery of foundational realities—defining truths, thirty-year trademarks, biblical touchstones—that had profoundly shaped what that church had been for the previous three decades.

Today, just as strongly as when I delivered those messages, I still see the summary of foundational, world-changing truths in this book more like a launch than a land. They lead us to pursue preparation rather than ponder consummation, to lay hold on the greater things to come rather than linger over the great things of the past.

The reason is that these foundational realities, expounded in each chapter, are wildly untamable, explosively uncontainable, and electrically future-creating. They don't just sustain the present and explain the past—they are living and active and supernaturally supercharged to take God's people to places we have not yet dreamed, in ways we have not yet dreamed.

And so we turn to this battery of foundational realities—these defining truths, these 30-year trademarks, these biblical touchstones—truths that have not merely shaped one church, but have turned the world upside down since the first days of Christianity, are still doing so today, and will continue to do so until Christ returns. We turn to wildly untamable, explosively uncontainable, electrically future-creating realities. We turn to be astonished by God.

God Absolutely Is

The first of these truths is that *God is*. Or to say it after the way our text puts it, *God is who he is*. Or to say it more philosophically, *God absolutely is.* This is the most basic fact and the most ultimate fact. Period. Of the billions of facts that there are, this one is at the bottom and at the top. It is the foundation of all others and the consummation of all others. Nothing is more basic and nothing is more ultimate than the fact that *God is.*

Nothing is more foundational than that *God is.* Nothing is more foundational to your life or your marriage or your job or your health or your mind or your future than that *God is.* Nothing is more foundational to the world, or the solar system, or the Milky Way, or the universe than that *God is.* And nothing is more foundational to the Bible, and the self-revelation of God, and the glory of the gospel of Jesus than that *God is.*

The reality that *God absolutely is* stands as the point of Exodus 3:13–15. Let me set the stage for you. For several centuries the people of Israel—God's chosen people— have lived as aliens in Egypt. And for a long time they have been treated as slaves. Now, as the time of God's deliverance is drawing near, a Jewish child is born, who will be given the name Moses. He is providentially rescued from an edict of death by Pharaoh's daughter and raised in the royal court. As an adult, while defending one of his kinsmen, he kills an Egyptian and then flees to the land of Midian. There, God appears to him in a burning bush.

> He said, "I am the God of your father, the God of Abraham, the God of Isaac, and the God of Jacob." And Moses hid his face, for he was afraid to look at God. [7] Then the LORD said, "I have surely seen the affliction of my people who are in Egypt and have heard their cry because

of their taskmasters. I know their sufferings, [8]
and I have come down to deliver them out of
the hand of the Egyptians and to bring them
up out of that land to a good and broad land, a
land flowing with milk and honey, to the place of
the Canaanites, the Hittites, the Amorites, the
Perizzites, the Hivites, and the Jebusites. [9] And
now, behold, the cry of the people of Israel has
come to me, and I have also seen the oppression
with which the Egyptians oppress them. [10] Come,
I will send you to Pharaoh that you may bring
my people, the children of Israel, out of Egypt."
(Exodus 3:6-10)

So Moses is chosen by God to lead his people out of
slavery and into the Promised Land, but he shrinks back,
as well might anyone. "But Moses said to God, 'Who am
I that I should go to Pharaoh and bring the children of
Israel out of Egypt?'" (v. 11). And God said, "But I will be
with you, and this shall be the sign for you, that I have sent
you: when you have brought the people out of Egypt, you
shall serve God on this mountain" (v. 12).

And then Moses brings us to one of the most important things God ever said.

Three Things God Says about Himself

Let's take another look at our text.

Then Moses said to God, "If I come to the
people of Israel and say to them, 'The God of
your fathers has sent me to you,' and they ask me,

'What is his name?' what shall I say to them?" ¹⁴
God said to Moses, "I AM WHO I AM." And he
said, "Say this to the people of Israel: 'I AM has
sent me to you.'" ¹⁵ God also said to Moses, "Say
this to the people of Israel: 'The LORD [Hebrew:
"Yahweh"], the God of your fathers, the God
of Abraham, the God of Isaac, and the God
of Jacob, has sent me to you.' This is my name
forever [Yahweh], and thus I am to be remembered throughout all generations." (Exodus
3:13–15)

You ask me my name, God says, so I will tell you three
things. First, "God said to Moses, 'I AM WHO I AM.'" (v.
14a). He did not say that was his name. He said, in effect,
"Before you worry about my name, or where I line up
among the many gods of Egypt or Babylon or Philistia,
and before you wonder about conjuring me with my name,
and even before you wonder if I Am the God of Abraham,
be stunned by this: *I Am Who I Am.* I absolutely am. Before
you get my name, get my being."

That "I Am Who I Am"—that *I absolutely Am*—is
first, foundational, and of infinite importance.

Second, "And he said, 'Say this to the people of Israel:
"I AM has sent me to you."'" (v. 14b). Notice that God is still
not telling Moses his name. He is building a bridge between
his being and his name, by putting the statement of his
being in the place of his name. Say, "I Am has sent me to
you." The one who is—who absolutely is—sent me to you.

Third, "God also said to Moses, 'Say this to the people
of Israel: "The LORD [Hebrew: "Yahweh"], the God of
your fathers, the God of Abraham, the God of Isaac, and

the God of Jacob, has sent me to you.' This [Yahweh] is my name forever." (v. 15). Finally, he gives us his name. It's almost always translated LORD in the English Bible. But the Hebrew would be pronounced something like "Yahweh," and is built on the word for "I Am." So every time you hear the word Yahweh (or the short form Yah—which you hear every time you sing "hallelu-jah"("praise Yahweh")—every time you see LORD in the English Bible, with those distinctive small capital letters, you should think: *this is a proper name* (like Jason or Melissa) *built out of the word for "I Am" and reminding us that God absolutely is.*

God absolutely is. This is amazing. God gave himself a name (used more than four thousand times in the Old Testament) that presses us, when we hear it, to think, *he is. He absolutely is. He is absolute.*

This is the first of the wildly untamable, explosively uncontainable, electrically future-creating realities we will discuss. A people who are stunned and astonished that *God is* will be an irrepressible people. Our triune God loves to show up in gracious power where people are blown away by the fact that he is.

Ten Things It Means for God to Be Who He Is

What does it mean for God to be who he is? Here are ten points:

1. *God's absolute being means he never had a beginning.* This staggers the mind. Every child asks, "Who made God?" And every wise parent says, "Nobody made God. God simply is. And always was. No beginning."

2. *God's absolute being means God will never end.* If he did not come into being, he cannot go out of being, because he *is* being. He is what is. There is no place to go outside of being. There is only he. Before he creates, that's all that is: God.

3. *God's absolute being means God is absolute reality.* There is no reality before him. There is no reality outside of him unless he wills it and makes it. Before he creates, he is not one of many realities. He is simply there as absolute reality. He is all that was eternally. No space, no universe, no emptiness. Only God. Absolutely there. Absolutely all.

4. *God's absolute being means that God is utterly independent.* He depends on nothing to bring him into being or support him or counsel him or make him what he is. That is what *absolute being* means.

5. *God's absolute being means that everything that is not God depends totally on God.* All that is not God is secondary and dependent. The entire universe is utterly secondary. Not primary. It came into being by God and stays in being moment-by-moment on God's decision to keep it in being.

6. *God's absolute being means all the universe is, by comparison to God, as nothing.* Contingent, dependent reality is to absolute, independent reality as a shadow to substance. As an echo to a thunderclap. As a bubble to the ocean. All that we see, all that we are amazed by in the world and in the galaxies is, compared to God, as nothing. "All the nations are as nothing before him, they are accounted by him as less than nothing and emptiness" (Isaiah 40:17).

7. *God's absolute being means that God is constant.* He is

the same yesterday, today, and forever. He cannot be improved. He is not becoming anything. He is who he is. There is no development in God. No progress. Absolute perfection cannot be improved upon.

8. *God's absolute being means that he is the absolute standard of truth and goodness and beauty.* There is no law book to which he looks to know what is right. No almanac to consult to establish facts. No guild to inquire of to determine what is excellent or beautiful. He himself is the standard of what is right, what is true, what is beautiful.

9. *God's absolute being means God does whatever he pleases and it is always right and always beautiful and always in accord with truth.* There are no constraints on him from outside him that could hinder him in doing anything he pleases. All reality that is outside of him he created and designed and governs as the absolute reality. So he is utterly free from any constraints that don't originate from the counsel of his own will.

10. *God's absolute being means that he is the most important and most valuable reality and the most important and most valuable person in the universe.* He is more worthy of interest and attention and admiration and enjoyment than all other realities, including the entire universe.

Because He Is

God absolutely is! Let us believe and cherish this. God is. It is a wildly untamable, explosively uncontainable, electrically future-creating reality—that God is. And it is a cosmic outrage billions of times over that he is ignored, treated as negligible, questioned, criticized, and given less consideration than the carpet in people's homes.

With God being the most significant reality, nothing is rightly known apart from its relationship to him. He is the source and goal and definer of all beings and all things. Let us, therefore, be a God-besotted people. To know him, to admire him, to make him known as glorious should be our driving passion. Let him be simply and overwhelmingly dominant in our consciousness. If we exist to spread a passion for the supremacy of God, then everything must start and end with him, everything must be related to him.

Therefore, God helping us, we will not blaspheme him. We will not blaspheme the God who absolutely is by taking him for granted, or making him peripheral, or calling him the assumed foundation of all the things while it's actually the "things" we are most excited about. Let us dread ever falling under the criticism of Albert Einstein that Charles Misner wrote about twenty years ago.

> I do see the design of the universe as essentially a religious question. That is, one should have some kind of respect and awe for the whole business.... It's very magnificent and shouldn't be taken for granted. In fact, I believe that is why Einstein had so little use for organized religion, although he strikes me as a basically very religious man. He must have looked at what the preachers said about God and felt that they were blaspheming. He had seen much more majesty than they had ever imagined, and they were just not talking about the real thing. (Quoted in *First Things*, Dec. 1991, No. 18, 63)

When I first read that quote I thought, *O God, never, never let that happen at our church!* I knew then, and I know now, that billions of people in the world are starving to know the true and living God who absolutely is. And we, who have the good news, know that this God has sent his Son into the world to die for God-belittling sinners like us, so that whoever believes in Jesus Christ may know this God, with joy, forever. So let us be fully aware of our calling as Christians. We exist to spread a passion for God who absolutely is.

You see, then, why I call this an untamable, uncontainable, electrically future-creating reality. "I Am Who I Am," he declares, now and forever. God absolutely is.

More about the God Who Is

GOD, GLORY, GOSPEL

> *In the year that King Uzziah died I saw the* Lord *sitting upon a throne, high and lifted up; and the train of his robe filled the temple. Above him stood the seraphim. Each had six wings: with two he covered his face, and with two he covered his feet, and with two he flew. And one called to another and said: "Holy, holy, holy is the* Lord *of hosts; the whole earth is full of his glory!" And the foundations of the thresholds shook at the voice of him who called, and the house was filled with smoke. —*Isaiah 6:1–4

Glimpse with me seven glorious truths about God in these four verses. And all of them follow from the fact that *God is.*

God Is Alive

In the year that King Uzziah died…

Just as God *is*, he is *alive*. Uzziah is dead, but God lives on. "From everlasting to everlasting, thou art God" (Psalm 90:2). God was the living God when this universe banged into existence. He was the living God when Socrates drank his poison. He was the living God when William Bradford governed Plymouth Colony. He was the living God in 1966 when Thomas Altizer proclaimed him dead and *Time* magazine put it on the front cover. And he will be the living God ten trillion ages from now when all the puny potshots against his reality will have sunk into oblivion like BBs at the bottom of the Pacific Ocean.

"In the year that King Uzziah died I saw the LORD." There is not a single head of state in all the world who will be there in fifty years. The turnover in world leadership is 100 percent. But not God. He never had a beginning and therefore depends on nothing for his existence. He always has been and always will be alive.

God Is Authoritative

I saw the LORD sitting upon a throne.

No vision of heaven has ever caught a glimpse of God plowing a field or cutting his grass or shining his shoes or filling out reports or loading a truck. Heaven is not coming apart at the seams by inattention. God is never at wit's end with his heavenly realm. He sits. And he sits on a *throne*. All is at peace and he has control.

The throne is his right to rule the world. We do not *give* God authority over our lives. He has it whether we like it or not. What utter folly it is to act as though we had any rights at all to call God into question! We need to hear, now and then, blunt words like those of Virginia Stem Owens who said in the *Reformed Journal*:

> Let us get this one thing straight. God can do anything he damn well pleases, including damn well. And if it pleases him to damn, then it is done, ipso facto, well. God's activity is what it is. There isn't anything else. Without it there would be no being, including human beings presuming to judge the Creator of everything that is.

Few things are more humbling, and few things give us that sense of raw majesty, than the truth that God is utterly authoritative. He is the Supreme Court, the Legislature, and the Chief Executive. After him, there is no appeal.

God Is Omnipotent
I saw the LORD sitting upon a throne high and lifted up.

The throne of God's authority is not one throne among many. It is high and lifted up. That God's throne is higher than every other throne signifies God's superior power to exercise his authority. No opposing authority can nullify the decrees of God. What he purposes, he accomplishes. "My counsel shall stand, and I will accomplish all my purpose" (Isaiah 46:10).

"He does according to his will in the host of heaven and among the inhabitants of the earth; and none can stay his hand" (Daniel 4:35). And this sovereign authority of the living God is a refuge full of joy and power for those who keep his covenant.

God Is Resplendent

I saw the LORD *sitting upon a throne high and lifted up, and his train filled the temple.*

You have seen pictures of brides whose dresses are gathered around them, covering the steps and the platform. What would the meaning be if the train filled the aisles and covered the seats and the choir loft, woven all of one piece? That God's robe fills the entire heavenly temple means that he is a God of incomparable splendor. The fullness of God's splendor shows itself in a thousand ways.

There are species of fish that live deep in the dark sea and have their own built-in lights—some have lamps hanging from their chins, some have luminescent noses, some have beacons under their eyes. There are a thousand kinds of these self-lighted fish living deep in the ocean where none of us can see and marvel. They are spectac-ularly weird and beautiful. Why are they there? And why not just a dozen or so efficient, streamlined models? Because God is lavish in splendor. His creative fullness spills over in excessive beauty. And if that's the way the world is, how much more resplendent must be the Lord who thought it up and made it!

God Is Revered

Above him stood the seraphim. Each had six wings: with two he covered his face, and with two he covered his feet, and with two he flew.

No one knows what these strange six-winged creatures with feet and eyes and intelligence are. They never appear again in the Bible, at least not under the name seraphim. Given the grandeur of the scene and the power of the angelic hosts, we had best not picture chubby, winged babies fluttering about God's ears. According to verse 4, when one of these beings speak, the foundations of the temple shake. We would do a little better to think of those thundering aerobatic fighter jets, the Blue Angels, diving in formation before a presidential entourage and cracking the sound barrier just as they pass by. There are no puny or silly creatures in heaven. Only magnificent ones.

And the point is that not even the seraphim can look upon the Lord, nor do they feel worthy even to leave their feet exposed in his presence. Great and good as they are, untainted by sin or the fall, they revere their Maker in great humility. An angel terrifies a man with his brilliance and power. But angels themselves hide in holy fear and reverence from the splendor of God. He is continually revered.

God Is Holy
> And one called to another and said: "Holy, holy, holy
> is the LORD of hosts!"

Language is pushing the limits of its usefulness here, and the effort to define the holiness of God ultimately winds up by saying that "God is holy" simply means "God is God." Let me illustrate.

The root meaning of holy is probably to *cut* or *separate*. A holy thing is something cut off and separated from common (we might say secular) use. Earthly things and persons are holy insofar as they are distinct from the world and devoted to God. So the Bible speaks of holy ground (Exodus 3:5), holy assemblies (Exodus 12:16), holy sabbaths (Exodus 16:23), a holy nation (Exodus 19:6), holy garments (Exodus 28:2), a holy city (Nehemiah 11:1), holy promises (Psalm 105:42), holy men (2 Peter 1:21) and women (1

Peter 3:5), holy Scriptures (2 Timothy 3:15), holy hands (1 Timothy 2:8), a holy kiss (Romans 16:16), and a holy faith (Jude 20). Almost anything can become holy if it is separated from the common and devoted to God.

But notice what happens when this definition is applied to God himself. From what can you separate God to make him holy? The very God-ness of God means he is separate from all that is not God. There is an infinite qualitative difference between Creator and creature. God is one-of-a-kind, *sui generis*, in a class by himself. In that sense he is utterly holy. But then you have said no more than that he is God!

Or if the holiness of a man derives from being separated from the world and devoted to God, to whom is God devoted so as to derive his holiness? To no one but himself. It is blasphemy to say that there is a higher reality than God to which he must conform in order to be holy. God is the absolute reality beyond which is only more of God. As we have seen, when asked for his name in Exodus 3:14, he said, "I AM WHO I AM." His being and his character are utterly undetermined by anything outside himself. He is not holy because he keeps the rules. He wrote the rules! God is not holy because he keeps the law. The law is holy because it reveals God. God is absolute. Everything else is derivative.

What then is his holiness? It is his infinite worth. His holiness is his utterly unique divine essence, which in his uniqueness has infinite value. It determines all that he is and does and is determined by no one. His holiness is what he is as God, which no one else is or ever will be. Call it his majesty, his divinity, his greatness, his value as the pearl of great price.

In the end, language runs out. In the word *holy* we have sailed to the world's end in the utter silence of reverence and wonder and awe. There may yet be more to know of God, but that will be beyond words. "The Lord is in his holy temple; let all the earth keep silence before him" (Habakkuk 2:20).

God Is Glorious

> *Holy, holy, holy is the Lord of hosts, the whole earth is full of his glory!*

But before the silence and the shaking of the foundations and the all-concealing smoke, we learn a seventh and final thing about God—he is glorious.

The glory of God is the manifestation of his holiness. God's holiness is the incomparable perfection of his divine nature; his glory is the display of that holiness. "God is glorious" means God's holiness has gone public. His glory is the open revelation of the secret of his holiness. When God shows himself to be holy, what we see is glory. The holiness of God is his concealed glory. The glory of God is his revealed holiness.

Connections between God and the Gospel

Now, what does all this—about a living, authoritative, omnipotent, resplendent, revered, holy, glorious God— have to do with the gospel of Jesus Christ, incarnate as the God-man, crucified and risen from the dead at the center of history? John, in chapter 12 of his gospel, makes the connections for us more clearly than anyone. Let's look at four of these connections very briefly.

First, in Isaiah 6:1–4, as we have just seen, Isaiah presents God on his throne. In verses 9–10, however, it says that this message of a glorious God will harden the people. They do not want a God of such majesty. Nevertheless, the chapter ends with a reference to a stump of faithfulness that remains, and Isaiah speaks of a "holy seed" (v. 13).

Then, in Isaiah 53, that seed is described as the suffering servant who had "no form or majesty that we should look at him, and no beauty that we should desire him. He was despised and rejected by men" (Isaiah 53:2–3).

So in Isaiah 6 we have majesty, authority, and power. But Isaiah 53 presents just the opposite—no majesty, no beauty, nothing desirable, just misery. Yet *both messages are rejected*: "Who has believed what he has heard from us?" (Isaiah 53:1). Whether glorious and sovereign, or humble and suffering, the result is the same: man rejects God.

Now, notice that the two Isaiah verses (53:1 and 6:10) are the very two texts that John quotes in reference to *the rejection of Jesus* (see John 12:38 and 40). Why these texts? John tells us, "Isaiah said these things because he saw his glory and spoke of him" (John 12:41).

In other words, Jesus was the fulfillment of both Isaiah passages—he was the enthroned Sovereign *and* the suffering servant. "And we have seen his glory, glory as of the only Son from the Father, full of grace and truth" (John 1:14), and that glory was the unprecedented mingling of the majesty of Isaiah 6 and the misery of Isaiah 53. "He came to his own, and his own people did not receive him" (John 1:11).

Why? Why was this incomparable Christ rejected? Again, John answers our question. The people "loved the glory that comes from man more than the glory that comes from God" (John 12:43). Because they loved human glory more than divine glory, they rejected Jesus—the embodiment of the glory of God, both in his greatness as God and his lowliness as the suffering servant.

All this was part of God's design. "The Son of Man came not to be served but to serve, and to give his life as a ransom for many" (Matthew 20:28; Mark 10:45). His rejection was the plan. Because his death for sinners was the plan.

Does God then abandon his people Israel because they rejected him? No. That too is part of the plan. "A partial hardening has come upon Israel, until the fullness of the Gentiles has come in. And in this way all Israel will be saved" (Romans 11:25–26). Or as Romans 11:31 says, "So they [Israel] too has been disobedient in order that by the mercy shown to you Gentiles they also may now receive mercy."

Nothing has been wasted. There were no detours on the way to this great salvation of all God's elect. So when Paul stands back and looks at the whole plan, he worships.

> Oh, the depth of the riches and wisdom and knowledge of God! How unsearchable are his judgments and how inscrutable his ways! "For who has known the mind of the Lord, or who has been his counselor? Or who has given a gift to him that he might be repaid?" For from him and through him and to him are all things. To him be glory forever. Amen." (Romans 11:33–36)

This is our God.

ISAIAH 43:1-7

But now thus says the LORD, he who created you, O Jacob, he who formed you, O Israel: "Fear not, for I have redeemed you; I have called you by name, you are mine. ² When you pass through the waters, I will be with you; and through the rivers, they shall not overwhelm you; when you walk through fire you shall not be burned, and the flame shall not consume you. ³ For I am the LORD your God, the Holy One of Israel, your Savior. I give Egypt as your ransom, Cush and Seba in exchange for you. ⁴ Because you are precious in my eyes, and honored, and I love you, I give men in return for you, peoples in exchange for your life. ⁵ Fear not, for I am with you; I will bring your offspring from the east, and from the west I will gather you. ⁶ I will say to the north, Give up, and to the south, Do not withhold; bring my sons from afar and my daughters from the end of the earth, ⁷ everyone who is called by my name, whom I created for my glory, whom I formed and made."

2
The Glory of God

After asking in chapter 1, "Who is God and what is his name?"—to which God answers, "I Am"—we find our next wildly untamable, explosively uncontainable, electrically future-creating reality in answer to the question, "Why did God create the world?"

The short answer, which resounds through the whole Bible like rolling thunder, is that *God created the world for his glory*. We'll talk in a moment about what that means, but let's establish the fact first.

Notice the key verses in Isaiah 43:6–7, "Bring my sons from afar and my daughters from the end of the earth, everyone who is called by my name, whom *I created for my glory*, whom I formed and made." Even if the narrowest meaning here is, "I brought Israel into being for my glory," the use of *created, formed*, and *made* are pointing us back to the original act of creation. This is why Israel *ultimately* exists. Because this is why *all* things ultimately exist—for the glory of God.

Created for His Glory

When the first chapter of the Bible says, "So God created man *in his own image*, in the *image of God* he created him; male and female he created them" (Genesis 1:27), what is the point? The point of an image is *to image*. Images are formed to express something about the original. Point to the original. Glorify the original. God made humans in his image so that the world would be filled with reflectors of God. Images of God. Many billions of statues of God. So that nobody would miss the point of creation, the point of humanity—knowing, loving, and showing God.

The angels cry, "Holy, holy, holy is the LORD of hosts; *the whole earth is full of his glory!*" (Isaiah 6:3). This earth is full of divine image-bearers, glorious ruins. And not only humans—also nature! Why such a breathtaking world for us to live in? Why such a vast universe? I read once that there are more stars in the universe than there are words and sounds that all humans of all time have ever spoken. Why?

The Bible is crystal clear about this: "The heavens declare the glory of God" (Psalm 19:1). Someone may ask, "If earth is the only inhabited planet and man the only rational inhabitant among the stars, why such a large and empty universe?" The answer is, because it's not about us. It's about God. And that's an understatement. God created us to know him and love him and show him. And then he gave us a hint of what he is like. That hint is the universe. The universe is declaring the glory of God, and the reason we exist is to see it and be stunned by it and glorify God because of it.

On this point, Paul writes, "His invisible attributes,

namely, his eternal power and divine nature, have been clearly perceived, ever since the creation of the world, in the things that have been made. So they are without excuse. For although they knew God, they did not honor him as God or give thanks to him" (Romans 1:20–21). The great tragedy of the universe is that while human beings were made to glorify God, we have all fallen short of this purpose and "exchanged the glory of the immortal God for images resembling mortal man" (Romans 1:23)—especially the one in the mirror. This is the essence of what we call sin.

So, why did God create the universe? Resounding through the whole Bible, from eternity to eternity, like rolling thunder, is the fact that God created the world for his glory.

Isaiah's Testimony

Isaiah states plainly that God created the world for his glory (v. 7). He goes on to press home the reality over and over to help us feel it and make it part of the fabric of our thinking.

> Every valley shall be lifted up, and every mountain and hill be made low; ... And *the glory of the Lord shall be revealed*, and all flesh shall see it together, for the mouth of the Lord has spoken. (Isaiah 40:4–5)

> I am the Lord; that is my name; my glory I give to no other, nor my praise to carved idols. (Isaiah 42:8)

> Break forth into singing, O mountains, O forest,

and every tree in it! For the LORD has redeemed
Jacob, and will be glorified in Israel. (Isaiah
44:23)

For my name's sake I defer my anger, for the
sake of my praise I restrain it for you… I have
tried you in the furnace of affliction. For my own
sake, for my own sake, I do it, for how should
my name be profaned? My glory I will not give
to another. (Isaiah 48:9–11)

And he said to me, 'You are my servant, Israel, in
whom I will be glorified.' (Isaiah 49:3)

For behold, darkness shall cover the earth, and
thick darkness the peoples; but the LORD will
arise upon you, and his glory will be seen upon
you. (Isaiah 60:2)

The Spirit of the LORD GOD is upon me, because
the LORD has anointed me to bring good news
to the poor; … to give them… the garment of
praise instead of a faint spirit; that they may be
called oaks of righteousness, the planting of the
LORD, that he may be glorified. (Isaiah 61:1–3)

What *Glorify* Means

God created the world, "that he may be glorified." This
does not mean "that he may be *made* glorious." Don't take
glorify and treat it like *beautify*. "Beautify" means to take a
plain room, for example, and make it beautiful. We don't
take a plain God and *make* him beautiful. That is not what
glorifying God means.

When God created the world, he did not create out of any need or weakness or deficiency. He created out of fullness and strength and complete sufficiency. As Jonathan Edwards said, "Tis no argument of the emptiness or deficiency of a fountain that it is inclined to overflow" (Yale: *Works*, Vol. 8, 448). So we don't glorify God by improving his glory, but by seeing and savoring and showing his glory (which is the same as knowing and loving and showing it).

Or consider the word *magnify* (so Philippians 1:20, "that Christ be magnified" [*megalunthesetai*], ASV, KJV, NKJV). We magnify God's glory like a telescope, not a microscope. Microscopes make small things look bigger than they are. Telescopes make unimaginably big but distant things look more like what they really are. Our lives are to be telescopes for the glory of God. We were created to see his glory, to be thrilled by his glory, and to live so as to help others see him and savor him for who and what he really is.

To know, to love, to show God's glory—this is why the universe exists. If this takes hold of you the way it should, it will affect the way you think and feel about everything. Because now you know why everything exists. You don't know everything—there are countless things you don't know—but you are never at a loss to know something important about everything, because you know that everything exists for the glory of God. And so to know this one thing—that all things exist for the glory of God—is to know something supremely important about everything. You know for what purpose it ultimately exists. That is amazing.

Glory Centered in the Cross

At the same time, to simply say that God created the world for his glory is too general a statement. We can't leave it there. It's too disconnected from the persons of the Trinity and from the flow of history as God is guiding it. The question is not merely, "Why did God create the world?" but why *this* world?—why these thousands of years of human history with a glorious beginning, and a horrible fall into sin, and the history of Israel, and the coming of the Son of God into the world, and then a substitutionary death, a triumphant resurrection, the founding of the church, and the history of global missions to where we are today? Why *this* world? This history?

The short answer is, *for the glory of God's grace displayed and revealed supremely in the saving death of Jesus.* Or to say it more fully: this world—this history as it is unfolding—was created and is being guided and sustained by God so that the grace of God, supremely displayed in the death and resurrection of Jesus for sinners, would be glorified throughout all eternity in the Christ-exalting joys of the redeemed.

Which means that being *God-centered* is, necessarily and specifically, to be *Christ-exalting* and to be *gospel-driven.* There is an eternally unbreakable connection between the glory of God, the glory of grace, the glory of Christ, and the glory of the cross. Indeed, everything in creation exists for the glory of God's grace displayed and revealed supremely in the saving death of Jesus.

Let's see how God's glory is connected to the cross of Christ. We can do it in five steps.

The Apex of God's Display of His Own Glory Is the Display of His Grace, Resulting in Praise

God "predestined us for adoption as sons through Jesus Christ, according to the purpose of his will, to the praise of his glorious grace" (Ephesians 1:5–6). In other words, the glory of God's *grace*—what Paul calls "the immeasurable riches of his grace in kindness toward us in Christ Jesus" (Ephesians 2:7)—is the high point and end point in the revelation of God's glory. And the aim of predestination is that we live to the praise of the glory of this grace forever.

This is the end point of God's glory. Everything else, even his wrath, serves this end, for Paul says, "Desiring to show his wrath and to make known his power, [God] has endured with much patience vessels of wrath… *in order to make known the riches of his glory for vessels of mercy*" (Romans 9:22–23). Wrath is penultimate. The glory of God's grace on the vessels of his mercy—that is ultimate.

God Planned the Praise of the Glory of His Grace before Creation

God "chose us in him *before the foundation of the world*… to the praise of his glorious grace" (Ephesians 1:4, 6). Grace was not an afterthought in response to the fall of man. It was the plan, because grace is the summit of the mountain of God's glory. And he created the world for his glory. He planned the world for the glory of his grace.

God's Plan Was That the Praise of the Glory of His Grace Would Come About through Jesus

"He predestined us for adoption to himself as sons *through Jesus Christ*… to the praise of his glorious grace" (Ephesians 1:5–6). This predestination to the praise of the glory of God's grace happened "through Jesus Christ." In the eternal fellowship of the Trinity, the Father and the Son planned that God's grace would be supremely revealed through the saving work of the Son.

Again, Paul says, God "called us to a holy calling, not because of our works but because of his own purpose and *grace*, which he gave us *in Christ Jesus* before the ages began" (2 Timothy 1:9). So, before the ages of time began, the plan was for the revelation of the glory of the grace of God, specifically through Christ Jesus.

From Eternity, God's Plan Was That the Glory of God's Grace Would Reach Its High Point in the Saving Work of Jesus

We see this in the name that was already stamped on the cover of the book of the redeemed before the creation of the world. Before there was any human sin to die for, God planned that his Son be slain for sinners. We know this because, before creation, a name was given to the book of life. Revelation 13:8 tells us that "everyone whose name has not been written before the foundation of the world in *the book of life of the Lamb who was slain*" will become a worshiper of the beast.

Before creation, the name of the book was "the book of life of the Lamb who was slain." The plan was glory. The plan was grace. The plan was Christ. And the plan was death. And that death for sinners like us is the heart of the gospel, which is why Paul calls it "the gospel of the glory of Christ." (2 Corinthians 4:4).

Therefore, the Ultimate Purpose of Creating and Guiding and Sustaining This World is the Praise of the Glory of the Grace of God in the Crucifixion of His Son for Sinners

This is why Revelation shows that for all eternity we will sing "the song of the Lamb" (Revelation 15:3). We will say with white-hot admiration and praise, "Worthy are you to take the scroll and to open its seals, *for you were slain*, and by your blood you ransomed people for God from every tribe and language and people and nation" (Revelation 5:9). We will praise ten thousand things about our Savior. But we will not say anything more glorious than this: you were slain, and ransomed millions.

So we ask in conclusion, "Why did God create the world?" And we answer with the Scriptures: God created the world for his glory. God did not create out of need. He did not create the world out of a deficiency that needed to be made up. He was not lonely. He was supremely happy in the fellowship of the Trinity—Father, Son, and Holy Spirit. He created the world to put his glory on display that his people might know him and love him and show him.

And why did he create a world that would become like this world? A world that fell into sin? A world that exchanged his glory for the glory of images? Why would he permit and guide and sustain such a world? And we answer: *for the praise of the glory of the grace of God displayed supremely in the death of Jesus.*

Closing Questions

The ultimate reason for all things is the communication of the glory of God's grace, resulting in the eternal, happy praise of a redeemed multitude from every people and tongue and tribe and nation. All things are created and guided and sustained for the glory of God, which reaches its apex in the glory of his grace, which shines most brightly in the glory of Christ, which comes to focus most clearly in the glory of the cross. So I ask:

Is the glory of God the brightest treasure on the horizon of your future? Paul expressed the Christian heart in Romans 5:2, "We rejoice in hope of the glory of God."

Is the glory of grace the sweetest news to your guilty soul?

Is the glory of Christ in your life the present, personal embodiment of the grace of God?

Is the glory of the cross the saddest and happiest beauty to your redeemed soul?

More about the Glory of God

GOD'S COMMITMENT TO HIS NAME

The LORD will not forsake his people, for his great name's sake, because it has pleased the LORD to make you a people for himself. —1 Samuel 12:22

Clearly implied in this verse is the fact that God has pleasure in his *name*. When he chooses a people, it says, he chooses them "for himself," so that when he acts to spare them, he acts "for his great name's sake." Therefore, beneath and behind God's delight in choosing a people there is a deeper delight, namely, the pleasure God has in his own name.

What does it mean that God has pleasure in his name? It means that God has pleasure in his own perfections, in his own glory. The name of God in Scripture often means virtually the same thing as God's glorious, excellent character.

But it often means something slightly different—the glory of God *gone public*. So the name of God often refers to his reputation, his fame, his renown. This is the way we use *name* when we say someone is "making a name for himself." Or we may call something a "name brand," a brand with a reputation.

This is what I think Samuel means in 1 Samuel 12:22 when he says that God made Israel a people "for himself," and that he would not cast Israel off "for his great name's sake."

Let's look briefly at several other passages that bring out this idea of God's fame or reputation or renown.

God's Waistcloth

In the book of Jeremiah, God describes Israel as a waistcloth that had been chosen to highlight God's glory but had been found unusable. "For as the loincloth clings to the waist of a man, so I made the whole house of Israel and the whole house of Judah cling to me, declares the LORD, that they might be for me a people, a name, a praise, and a glory, but they would not listen" (Jeremiah 13:11).

Why was Israel chosen and made the garment of God? That it might be a "name, a praise, and a glory." In this context, *praise* and *glory* tell us that *name* means "renown" or "reputation." God chose Israel so that the people would make a reputation for him.

David's Teaching

David teaches the same thing in one of his prayers. He says that what sets Israel apart from all the other peoples is that God has dealt with them in such a way as to make a name for himself. "And who is like your people Israel, the one nation on earth whom God went to redeem to be his people, making himself a name and doing for them great and awesome things by driving out before your people, whom you redeemed for yourself from Egypt, a nation and its gods?" (2 Samuel 7:23).

In other words, when God went to redeem his people in Egypt and then bring them through the wilderness and into the Promised Land, he was not just favoring the people. He was acting, as Samuel says, for his own "great name's sake;" or, as David says, he was "making himself a name"—a reputation.

The Point of the Exodus

Let's go back to the exodus for a moment. This is where God really formed a people for himself. For the rest of her existence Israel has looked back to the exodus as the key event in her history. So in the exodus we can see what God is up to in choosing a people for himself.

In Exodus 9, God speaks to Pharaoh a word that lets him (and us) know why God is drawing out the deliverance to ten plagues, instead of making short work of it in one swift catastrophe. This text is so crucial that Paul quotes it in Romans 9:17 to sum up God's purpose in the exodus. God says to Pharaoh, "But for this purpose I have raised you up, to show you my power, so that my name may be proclaimed in all the earth" (Exodus 9:16).

The point of the exodus was to make a worldwide reputation for God. The point of the ten plagues and miraculous Red Sea crossing was to demonstrate the incredible power of God on behalf of his freely chosen people, with the aim that this reputation, this name, would be declared throughout the whole world. God has great pleasure in his reputation.

The Testimony of Isaiah

Did the later prophets and poets of Israel interpret the exodus that way? Yes, they did.

Isaiah says that God's aim in the exodus was to make for himself an everlasting name. He described God as the one,

> ...who caused his glorious arm to go at the right hand of Moses, who divided the waters before them to make for himself an everlasting name, who led them through the depths... Like a horse in the desert, they did not stumble. Like livestock that go down into the valley, the Spirit of the LORD gave them rest. So you led your people, to make for yourself a glorious name. (Isaiah 63:12–14)

So when God showed his power to deliver his people from Egypt through the Red Sea, he had his sights on eternity and the everlasting reputation that he would win for himself in those days.

The Teaching of the Psalms

Psalm 106 teaches the same thing. "Our fathers, when they were in Egypt, did not consider your wondrous works; they did not remember the abundance of your steadfast love, but rebelled by the sea, at the Red Sea. ⁸ Yet he saved them for his name's sake, that he might make known his mighty power" (Psalm 106:7–8).

Do you see the same gospel logic at work here that we saw in 1 Samuel 12:22? There the sinful people had chosen a king and angered God. But God does not cast them off. Why? "For his great name's sake." Here it says that the sinful people had rebelled against God at the Red Sea and failed to consider his love. Yet he saved them with tremendous power. Why? Same answer: "to make for yourself a glorious name."

Do you see that God's first love is his name and not his people? And precisely because of this, there is hope for his sinful people. Do you see why the God-centeredness of God is the ground of the gospel?

Joshua's Prayer

Take Joshua as another example of someone who understood this God-centered gospel logic and put it to use, like Moses did (Deuteronomy 9:27–29; Numbers 14:13–16), to plead for God's sinful people. In Joshua 7 Israel has crossed the Jordan, entered the Promised Land, and defeated Jericho. But now they have been defeated at Ai and Joshua is stunned. He goes to the Lord in one of the most desperate prayers in all the Bible. "O LORD, what can I say, when Israel has turned their backs before their enemies! For the Canaanites and all the inhabitants of the land will hear of it and will surround us and cut off our name from the earth. And what will you do for your great name?" (Joshua 7:8–9).

Do you cry for mercy on the basis of God's love for his name? The great ground of hope in all the God-centered servants of the Lord has always been the impossibility that God would let his great name be dishonored among the nations. It was inconceivable. This was bedrock confidence. Other things change, but not this—not the commitment of God to his name.

Ezekiel's Witness in Exile

But what, then, are we to make of the fact that eventually Israel proved to be so rebellious that she was indeed given into the hands of her enemies in the Babylonian captivity during the time of Ezekiel? How does a God-centered prophet like Ezekiel handle this terrible setback for the reputation of God?

Consider the word of the Lord that came to him in chapter 36. This is God's answer to the captivity of his people which he himself had brought about.

> But when they came to the nations, wherever they came, they profaned my holy name, in that people said of them, "These are the people of the LORD, and yet they had to go out of his land." But I had concern for my holy name, which the house of Israel had profaned among the nations to which they came. Therefore say to the house of Israel, Thus says the LORD GOD: It is not for your sake, O house of Israel, that I am about to act, but for the sake of my holy name, which you

have profaned among the nations to which you
came. And I will vindicate the holiness of my
great name, which has been profaned among the
nations, and which you have profaned among
them. And the nations will know that I am the
LORD, declares the Lord GOD, when through
you I vindicate my holiness before their eyes.
(Ezekiel 36:20–23)

When every other hope was gone, and the people lay under
the judgment of God himself because of their own sin, one
hope remained—and it will always remain—that God has
an indomitable delight in the worth of his own reputation,
and will not suffer it to be trodden down for long.

PHILIPPIANS 1:12–26

I want you to know, brothers, that what has happened to me has really served to advance the gospel, [13] so that it has become known throughout the whole imperial guard and to all the rest that my imprisonment is for Christ. [14] And most of the brothers, having become confident in the Lord by my imprisonment, are much more bold to speak the word without fear. [15] Some indeed preach Christ from envy and rivalry, but others from good will. [16] The latter do it out of love, knowing that I am put here for the defense of the gospel. [17] The former proclaim Christ out of selfish ambition, not sincerely but thinking to afflict me in my imprisonment. [18] What then? Only that in every way, whether in pretense or in truth, Christ is proclaimed, and in that I rejoice. Yes, and I will rejoice, [19] for I know that through your prayers and the help of the Spirit of Jesus Christ this will turn out for my deliverance, [20] as it is my eager expectation and hope that I will not be at all ashamed, but that with full courage now as always Christ will be honored in my body, whether by life or by death. [21] For to me to live is Christ, and to die is gain. [22] If I am to live in the flesh, that means fruitful labor for me. Yet which I shall choose I cannot tell. [23] I am hard pressed between the two. My desire is to depart and be with Christ, for that is far better. [24] But to remain in the flesh is more necessary on your account. [25] Convinced of this, I know that I will remain and continue with you all, for your progress and joy in the faith, [26] so that in me you may have ample cause to glory in Christ Jesus, because of my coming to you again.

3
Christian Hedonism

The term *Christian Hedonism* may be catchy and controversial, but it's not in the Bible. No one needs to like it just because I do. So the point of this chapter is not at all to push a label or a slogan, but to talk about the massive and pervasive biblical truth that some of us love to call Christian Hedonism.

This chapter is packed with some of the juiciest, most wonderful, most astonishing truths that I love to know and experience. Here's the outline.

- There's a problem that needs be solved relating to the glory of God.
- What we call Christian Hedonism is the solution to that problem.
- The apostle Paul and C.S. Lewis provide the basis for that solution.
- This solution—Christian Hedonism—changes every-

thing in your life, which I will try to show in eleven examples.

Is God's Self-Promotion Loveless?

In chapter two we asked, "Why did God create this world?" And the answer, "God created this world *for the praise of the glory of his grace displayed and revealed supremely in the saving death of Jesus.*" This poses a problem for some people—that at the heart of that answer is God's self-promotion; that God created the world for his own praise, for his own glory. (We addressed this somewhat in chapter two, but it deserves more detailed attention here.)

Oprah Winfrey, Brad Pitt, the early C.S. Lewis, Eric Reece, and Michael Prowse, among others, all walk away from such a God. They stumble over God's self-promotion.

> Oprah walked away from orthodox Christianity when she was about twenty-seven because of the biblical teaching that God is jealous—he demands that he and no one else get our highest allegiance and affection. It didn't sound loving to her.

> Brad Pitt turned away from his boyhood faith, he says, because God says, "You have to say that I'm the best.... It seemed to be about ego."

> C.S. Lewis, before he became a Christian, complained that God's demand to be praised sounded like "a vain woman who wants compliments."

> Erik Reece, the writer of *An American Gospel*,

> rejected the Jesus of the Gospels because only an egomaniac would demand that we love him more than we love our parents and children.

> Michael Prowse, columnist for the *London Financial Times*, turned away because only "tyrants, puffed up with pride, crave adulation."

So people can see this as a problem—that God created the world for his own praise. They think such self-exaltation would have to be immoral and loveless. That may be how you feel.

Christian Hedonism Offers the Answer

God is most glorified in you when you are most satisfied in him. That's the shortest summary of what we mean by Christian Hedonism. If that is true, however, then there is no conflict between your greatest exhilaration and God's greatest glorification.

In fact, not only is there no conflict between your happiness and God's glory, but his glory shines in your happiness, when your happiness is in him. And since God is the source of greatest happiness, and since he is the greatest Treasure in the world, and since his glory is the most satisfying gift he could possibly give us, therefore it is the kindest, most loving thing he could possibly do—to reveal himself and magnify himself and vindicate himself for our everlasting enjoyment. "In your presence there is fullness of joy; at your right hand are pleasures forever-more" (Psalm 16:11).

God is the one being for whom self-exaltation is the

most loving act, because he is exalting for us what alone can satisfy us, fully and forever. If we exalt ourselves, we are not loving, because we distract people from the one Person who can make them happy forever—God. But if God exalts himself, he draws attention to the one Person who can make us happy forever—himself. He is not an egomaniac. He is an infinitely glorious, all-satisfying God, offering us everlasting and supreme joy in himself.

That's the solution to our problem.

> No, Oprah: if God were not jealous for all your affections, he would be indifferent to your final misery.

> No, Brad Pitt: if God didn't demand that you see him as the best, he wouldn't care about your supreme happiness.

> No, Mr. Lewis: God is not vain in demanding your praise. This is his highest virtue, and your highest joy.

> No, Erik Reece: if Jesus didn't lay claim on greater love than your children do, he would be selling your heart to what cannot satisfy forever.

> No, Michael Prowse: God does not crave your adulation, he offers it as your greatest pleasure.

God is most glorified in you when you are most satisfied in him. God's motivation for pursuing his own glory turns out to be love. And our duty to pursue God's glory turns out to be a quest for joy. That's the solution to the problem of God's self-exaltation.

Reasonable and Biblical Basis

C.S. Lewis saw the basis for this in human experience. The apostle Paul shows it in his letter to the Philippians. Here is the great discovery as I first found it in Lewis's book, *Reflections on the Psalms*. He is discovering why God's demand for our praise is not vain.

> The most obvious fact about praise—whether of God or any thing—strangely escaped me. I thought of it in terms of compliment, approval, or the giving of honor. I had never noticed that all enjoyment spontaneously overflows into praise unless… shyness or the fear of boring others is deliberately brought in to check it. The world rings with praise—lovers praising their mistresses, readers their favorite poet, walkers praising the countryside, players praising their favorite game—praise of weather, wines, dishes, actors, motors, horses, colleges, countries, historical personages, children, flowers, mountains, rare stamps, rare beetles, even sometimes politicians or scholars. I had not noticed how the humblest, and at the same time most balanced and capacious, minds, praised most, while the cranks, misfits and malcontents praised least.…

> I had not noticed either that just as men spontaneously praise whatever they value, so they spontaneously urge us to join them in praising it: "Isn't she lovely? Wasn't it glorious? Don't you think that magnificent?" The Psalmists in telling everyone to praise God are doing what all men

do when they speak of what they care about. My whole, more general, difficulty about the praise of God depended on my absurdly denying to us, as regards the supremely Valuable, what we delight to do, what indeed we can't help doing, about everything else we value.

I think we delight to praise what we enjoy because the praise not merely expresses but completes the enjoyment; it is it's appointed consummation. It is not out of compliment that lovers keep on telling one another how beautiful they are; the delight is incomplete till it is expressed. (C.S. Lewis, *Reflections on the Psalms* [New York: Harcourt, Brace and World, 1958], 93–95.)

There it was. God's relentless command that we see him as glorious and praise him is a command that we settle for nothing less than the completion of our joy in him. Praise is not just the expression, but the consummation, of our joy in what is supremely enjoyable, namely, God. In *his* presence is fullness of joy; at *his* right hand are pleasures forevermore (Psalm 16:11). In demanding our praise, he is demanding the completion of our pleasure. God is most glorified in us when we are most satisfied in him.

That is also what we find in Philippians 1:20–23.

It is my eager expectation and hope that I will not be at all ashamed, but that with full courage now as always Christ will be honored in my body, whether by *life* or by *death*. [21] For to me to *live* is Christ, and to *die* is gain. [22] If I am to live

in the flesh, that means fruitful labor for me. Yet
which I shall choose I cannot tell. [23] I am hard
pressed between the two. My desire is to depart
and be with Christ, for that is far better.

Paul says that his great passion in life—I hope it's also
your great passion in life—is that in this life Christ be
seen as great, supremely great. That is why God created us
and saved us—to make Christ look like what he really is:
supremely great.

Now the relationship between verse 20 and 21 is the
key to seeing how Paul thinks that happens. Paul says that
Christ is going to be magnified in his body by life or death
"for to me to live is Christ and to die is gain" (v. 21). Notice
that *life* in verse 20 corresponds to *live* in verse 21, and
death in verse 20 corresponds to *die* in verse 21. So Paul is
explaining in both cases—life and death—how Christ is
going to look great.

He will look great in Paul's *life* because, "for to me to
live is Christ." He explains later in Philippians, "I count
everything as loss because of the surpassing worth of
knowing Christ Jesus my Lord" (3:8). So Christ is more
precious, more valuable, more satisfying than all that life
on this earth can give.

This is what Paul means when he says, "To me to live
is Christ" (v. 21). And *that* he says is how his life magnifies
Christ—makes Christ look great. Christ is most magnified in Paul's life when Paul, in his life, is most satisfied in
Christ. That's the plain teaching of these two texts.

And it gets even plainer when you consider the death
half of Philippians 1:20–23. Christ will be magnified in
Paul's body by death, "for to me... to die is gain" (v. 21).

Why would death be gain? The answer is at the end of verse 23. "My desire is to depart and be with Christ, for that is far better." Death is gain because it means a greater closeness of being with Christ. To experience death is "to depart and be with Christ."

This is why Paul says in verse 21 that to die is gain. You add up all the losses that death will cost you (your family, your job, your dream retirement, the friends you leave behind, your favorite bodily pleasures)—you add up all these losses, and then you replace them only with death and Christ—if when you do that you joyfully say, *gain!*, then Christ is magnified in your dying. Christ is most magnified in your death, when you are so satisfied in Christ, that losing everything and getting only Christ is called gain. Or to sum up both halves of the verse, *Christ is glorified in you when he is more precious to you than all that life can give and all that death can take.*

That's the biblical basis for the summary description of Christian Hedonism: God is most glorified in us when we are most satisfied in him. Notice that this was implicit in the previous chapter when we said that God created the world *for the praise of the glory of his grace displayed and revealed supremely in the saving death of Jesus.* In other words, God's pursuit of his own praise reaches its climax at the place where it does us the most good, the cross. At the cross God upholds his glory *and* provides our forgiveness. At the cross God vindicates his own honor *and* secures our happiness. At the cross God magnifies his own worth *and* satisfies our soul.

In the greatest act of history, Christ made it come true for undeserving sinners that God could be most glorified in us by our being most satisfied in him.

How Christian Hedonism Changes Everything

There are at least eleven areas in which Christian Hedonism fundamentally alters how we experience, process, and live this life.

Death

We've just seen how Christian Hedonism changes death. If you want to make Christ look great in your dying, no big performance or achievement or heroic sacrifice is required. All that's needed is a childlike laying yourself into the arms of the one who makes the loss of everything to be gain for those he calls his own.

Conversion

Christian Hedonism changes how we think about conversion. "The kingdom of heaven is like treasure hidden in a field, which a man found and covered up. Then in his joy he goes and sells all that he has and buys that field" (Matthew 13:44). Becoming a Christian not only means believing truth; it means finding a treasure. So evangelism becomes not only persuasion about truth but pointing people to a Treasure—one more valuable than everything they have.

The Fight of Faith

Christian Hedonism changes "the good fight of faith" (1 Timothy 6:12) into a fight for joy. John says, "To all who did *receive* [Jesus], who *believed* in his name, he gave the right to become children of God" (John 1:12). Believing Jesus is receiving him. Receiving him as what? As the infinitely valuable Treasure that he is. Faith is seeing and savoring this Treasure. And so the fight of faith is a fight for joy in Jesus. A fight to see and savor Jesus as more

precious than anything in the world. Because this savoring
shows him to be supremely valuable.

Combating Evil

Christian Hedonism changes how we combat evil in our
lives. Jeremiah 2:13 gives the Christian Hedonist definition
of evil—"My people have committed two evils: they have
forsaken me, the fountain of living waters, and hewed out
cisterns for themselves, broken cisterns that can hold no
water." Evil is the suicidal preference for the empty wells
of the world over the living waters of God's fellowship. We
fight evil by the pursuit of the fullest satisfaction in the
river of God's delights (Psalm 36:8).

What Hell Is

Christian Hedonism changes how we think of hell. Since
the way to be saved and go to heaven is to embrace Jesus
as your source of greatest joy, then hell is a place of suffering, of eternal unhappiness, prepared for people who refuse
to be happy in the triune God.

Self-Denial

Christian Hedonism changes the way we think about
self-denial. Self-denial really is there in the teachings
of Jesus, "If anyone would come after me, let him deny
himself and take up his cross and follow me" (Mark 8:34).
But now the meaning becomes:

> Deny yourself the wealth of the world so you can
> have the wealth of being with Christ.

> Deny yourself the fame and approval of the
> world to have the joy of God's approval.

> Deny yourself the security and safety of the

world to have the solid, secure fellowship of
Jesus.

Deny yourself the short, unsatisfying pleasures
of the world so that you can have fullness of joy
and pleasures forevermore at God's right hand.

Which means there is no such thing as ultimate self-denial.
Because to live is Christ and to die is gain. (Also see more
about self-denial at the end of this chapter.)

Money

Christian Hedonism changes the way we think about
handling our money and the act of giving. Acts 20:35 says,
"It is more blessed to give than to receive." And 2 Corinthians 9:7 says, "Each one must give as he has decided in his
heart, not reluctantly or under compulsion, for God loves a
cheerful giver." The motive to be a generous person is that
it expresses and expands our joy in God. And the pursuit
of deepest joy is the pursuit of giving, not getting.

Corporate Worship

Christian Hedonism changes the way we do corporate
worship. Corporate worship is the collective act of glorifying God. But God is glorified in a church service when
the people are satisfied in him. Therefore, the worship
leaders—musicians and preachers—see their task primarily
as breaking open a fountain of living water and spreading
a feast of rich food. The task of the worshipers is to drink
and eat and be satisfied. Because God is most glorified in
those worshipers when they are most satisfied in him.

Disability and Weakness

Christian Hedonism changes the way we experience disability and weakness. Stunningly, paradoxically, Jesus says to the weak and thorn-pierced Paul, "My grace is sufficient for you, for my power is made perfect in weakness." To which Paul responds, "Therefore I will boast all the more gladly [yes, this is the voice of the thorn-pierced Christian Hedonist] of my weaknesses, so that the power of Christ may rest upon me" (2 Corinthians 12:9).

Love
Christian Hedonism changes the meaning of love. Paul describes the love of the Macedonians like this: "In a severe test of affliction, their *abundance of joy* and their extreme poverty have overflowed in a wealth of generosity on their part" (2 Corinthians 8:2). In verse 8, Paul calls this "love." "Abundance of joy" in "a severe test of affliction" and "extreme poverty" overflowed in loving generosity. They were still poor, still afflicted, but so full of joy that it overflowed in love. So Christian Hedonism defines love as the overflow (or the expansion) of joy in God that meets the needs of others.

Ministry
Christian Hedonism changes the meaning of ministry. What is the ministry aim of the great apostle Paul? It is this: "Not that we lord it over your faith, but we work with for your joy, for you stand firm in your faith" (2 Corinthians 1:24). All ministry should be, by one means or another, a working with others for their joy.

That's why God created you. That's why Christ died for you. That's why pastors should serve. And that is why I speak and preach and write. I want to come alongside others in ministry as a worker with you for your joy in God. Because God is most glorified in you when you are most satisfied in him.

More about Christian Hedonism

EIGHT REASONS TO PURSUE YOUR SATISFACTION IN GOD

The *implications* of Christian Hedonism are numerous and pervasive. One of the biggest implications is that we should pursue our joy in God. *Should!* Not *may.* The main business of our hearts ought to be maximizing our satisfaction in God. *Not* our satisfaction in his gifts, no matter how good, but in him.

Here are eight biblical reasons to pursue your greatest and longest satisfaction in God. Some of these were noted earlier, but they are worth repeating here.

We Are Commanded to Do So

Serve the LORD with gladness! (Psalm 100:2)
Rejoice in the Lord always. (Philippians 4:4)
Delight yourself in the LORD. (Psalm 37:4)

We Are Threatened If We Don't

Because you did not serve the LORD your God with joyfulness and gladness of heart… therefore you shall serve your enemies. (Deuteronomy 28:47–48)

The Nature of Faith Teaches This Pursuit

Without faith it is impossible to please him, for whoever would draw near to God must believe that he exists and that he rewards those who seek him. (Hebrews 11:6)

The Nature of Evil Teaches This Pursuit

Be appalled, O heavens, at this; be shocked,

be utterly desolate, declares the LORD, for my people have committed two evils: they have forsaken me, the fountain of living waters, and hewed out cisterns for themselves, broken cisterns that can hold no water. (Jeremiah 2:12–13)

The Nature of Conversion Teaches This Pursuit

The kingdom of heaven is like treasure hidden in a field, which a man found and covered up. Then in his joy he goes and sells all that he has and buys that field. (Matthew 13:44)

The Call for Self-Denial Teaches This Pursuit

If anyone would come after me, let him deny himself and take up his cross and follow me. For whoever would save his life will lose it, but whoever loses his life for my sake and the gospel's will save it. For what does it profit a man to gain the whole world and forfeit his soul? (Mark 8:34–36)

The Demand to Love People Teaches This Pursuit

For the joy that was set before him [Jesus] endured the cross. (Hebrews 12:2)
It is more blessed to give than to receive. (Acts 20:35)

The Demand to Glorify God Teaches This Pursuit

It is my eager expectation and hope that... Christ will be [glorified] in my body, whether by life or by death. For to me to live is Christ, and to die is gain (final and total satisfaction in him). (Philippians 1:20–21)

Therefore, I invite you to join George Mueller, the great

prayer warrior and lover of orphans, in saying, "I saw more clearly than ever, that the first great and primary business to which I ought to attend every day was, to have my soul happy in the Lord." In this way, we will be able to suffer the loss of all things in the sacrifices of love, and "count it all joy."

Christian Self-Denial is Self-Interest

Someone may say, "How can you talk as if it is right to be motivated by a desire for our own good? How can you say, 'Make pleasure your aim,' when Jesus so clearly taught that we should deny ourselves and take up our cross?"

Well, if you think that's what Jesus taught, I have good news for you. Let's read the whole passage of Mark 8:34–36:

> If anyone would come after me, let him deny himself and take up his cross and follow me. For whoever would save his life will lose it, but whoever loses his life for my sake and the gospel's will save it. For what does it profit a man to gain the whole world and forfeit his soul?

The whole premise of this argument is hedonistic. Nobody wants to lose his life. There is no profit—no pleasure—in that. So here is how to save your life and have infinite joy—lose it in a life of love. Every sacrifice Jesus asks us to make, he asks us to make because he promises something vastly better. Self-denial? Sure, deny yourself the mud pie in the slum so you can have the holiday at the sea, as Lewis has said.

Jesus asked a rich young man once to deny himself, to sell everything he had, give it to the poor, and follow Jesus.

Now what do you think should have motivated that man to sell all his goods? Some kind of disinterested benevolence? The Bible does not know any such thing.

Jesus told two parables to show what the rich young man's motive should have been. "The kingdom of heaven is like treasure hidden in a field, which a man found and covered up. Then in *his joy* he goes and sells all that he has and buys that field" (Matthew 13:44). The rich young man should have sold all that he had because the prospect of following Jesus into the kingdom was so exciting and so joyful that all his possessions were of no comparison. "Again, the kingdom of heaven is like a merchant in search of fine pearls, who, on finding one pearl of great value, went and sold all that he had and bought it" (Matthew 13:45).

There is no such thing as ultimate self-sacrifice in the kingdom of God. Jesus asks us to renounce our little plastic beads of money and vain ambition and sensual pleasures because he has a real pearl for us. Even when his love was purest at Calvary, Jesus "endured the cross," as Hebrews 12:2 says, "for the *joy* that was set before him." Christian Hedonism is a way of saying that it is not best to do things under compulsion, because it is *cheerful* givers, *joyful* lovers, that the Lord seeks (2 Corinthians 9:7).

I once wrote a letter to one of my past students who disagreed with me on this. He had written me a note saying,

> I disagree with your position that love seeks or is motivated by its own pleasure... Are you familiar with Dorothy Day? She is a very old woman who has devoted her life to loving others, espe-

cially the poor, displaced, and downtrodden. Her experience of loving when there was no joy has led her to say that, "Love in action is a harsh and dreadful thing."

I responded in two ways. Here is the essence of that response.

First, don't jump to the conclusion that there is no joy in things that are "harsh and dreadful." There are mountain climbers who have spent sleepless nights on the faces of cliffs, have lost fingers and toes in subzero temperatures, and have gone through horrible misery to reach a peak. They freely admit the experience is harsh and dreadful. But if you ask them why they do it, the answer will come back in various forms that there is an accompanying exhilaration in the soul that feels so good it is worth all the pain.

If this is how it is with mountain climbing, cannot the same be true of love? Is it not rather an indictment of our own worldliness that we are more inclined to sense exhilaration in mountain climbing than in conquering the precipices of un-love in our own lives and in society? Yes, love is often a harsh and dreadful thing, but I do not see how a person who cherishes what is good and admires Jesus can help but feel a sense of joyful exhilaration when, by grace, he is able to love another person.

Now consider Dorothy Day's situation in another way. Let's pretend I am one of the poor that she is trying to help at great cost to herself. I think a conversation under those circumstances might go like this:

Piper: Why are you doing this for me, Miss Day?

Day: Because I love you.

Piper: What do you mean, you love me? I don't have anything to offer. I am not worth loving.

Day: Perhaps. But there are no application forms for my love. I learned that from Jesus. What I mean is I want to help you because Jesus has helped me so much.

Piper: So you are trying to satisfy your "wants?"

Day: I suppose so, if you want to put it like that. One of my deepest wants is to make you a happy and purposeful person.

Piper: Does it upset you that I am happier and that I feel more purposeful since you've come?

Day: Heavens no! What could make me happier!

Piper: So you really spend all these sleepless nights here for what makes you happy, don't you?

Day: If I say yes someone might misunderstand me. They might think I don't care for you at all, but only for myself.

Piper: But won't you say it at least for me?

Day: Yes, I'll say it for you: I work for what brings me the greatest joy—your joy.

Piper: Thank you. Now I know that you love me.

ISAIAH 46:8-11

Remember this and stand firm, recall it to mind, you transgressors, [9] remember the former things of old; for I am God, and there is no other; I am God, and there is none like me, [10] declaring the end from the beginning and from ancient times things not yet done, saying, 'My counsel shall stand, and I will accomplish all my purpose,' [11] calling a bird of prey from the east, the man of my counsel from a far country. I have spoken, and I will bring it to pass; I have purposed, and I will do it.

4

The Sovereignty
of God

We turn now to another truth that has turned the world upside down. This is our fourth wildly untamable, explosively uncontainable, and electrically future-creating reality; certainly one of the most foundational of the ten discussed in his book: the priceless truth of the sovereignty of God. Let's go right to our text, lest even from the beginning we import something that does not come from the word of God. This matter is far too serious, and touches on so many painful realities, that we dare not trust ourselves to arrive at truth without being told by God himself.

In Isaiah 46:9 God says, "I am God, and there is no other; I am God, and there is none like me." The focus in this text is the uniqueness of God among all the beings of the universe. He is in a class by himself. No one is like him. At issue here is what it means to be God. Twice in this verse, when he declares, "I am God!", it is as if he is saying,

"You're acting like you don't know what it means for me to be God!"

What It Means to Be God

So God then tells us what it means to be the one and only God. He tells us what's at the heart of his God-ness. *What it means for me to be God is that I declare "the end from the beginning and from ancient times things not yet done"* (Isaiah 46:10).

There are two statements here. First, God declares how things will turn out long before they ever happen ("from ancient times"). Second, God declares not just natural events but human events (things "not yet done"). That is, God knows what these doings will be long before they are done.

Now at this point you might say, "What we have here is the doctrine of God's foreknowledge, not the doctrine of his sovereignty." And that is right, so far. But in the second half of verse 10, God tells us *how* he foreknows the end and *how* he foreknows the things not yet done. "[I declare] the end from the beginning and from ancient times things not yet done, saying, 'My counsel shall stand, and I will accomplish all my purpose.'" When God "declares" ahead of time what will be, here's how he "declares" or "says" it: "saying, 'My counsel shall stand, and I will accomplish all my purpose.'"

In other words, the way God declares his fore-knowledge is by declaring his fore-counsel and his fore-purposing. When God declares the end long before it happens, what he says is, "My counsel shall stand." And when God declares things not yet done long before they are done, what he says is "I will accomplish all my purpose." Which means that *the reason God knows the future is because he plans the future and accomplishes it.* The future *is* the counsel of God being established. The future *is* the purpose of God being accomplished by God.

The next verse gives a clear confirmation that this is what he means. "I have spoken, and I will bring it to pass; I have purposed, and I will do it" (Isaiah 46:11). The reason God's predictions come true is because they are his purposes, and because he himself performs them.

God is not a fortuneteller, a soothsayer, a mere predictor. He doesn't have a crystal ball. He knows what's coming because he plans what's coming and he performs what he plans. "My counsel shall stand, and I will accomplish all my purpose" (v. 10b). He does not form purposes and then wonder if someone else will take responsibility to make them happen. "I will accomplish all my purpose."

So, based on this text, here's what I mean by the sovereignty of God: *God has the rightful authority, the freedom, the wisdom, and the power to bring about everything that he intends to happen. And therefore, everything he intends to come about does come about.*

This means that God plans and governs all things. When he says, "I will accomplish all my purpose," he means, "Nothing happens except what is my purpose." According to Isaiah 46:10-11, no other outcome is possible. Therefore, what God means in these two verses is that nothing has ever happened, or will ever happen, that God did not purpose to happen. Or to put it positively, everything that has happened or will happen has been purposed by God to happen.

Now if that seemed a little too complicated, let's do

something simpler. Let's confirm this view of God's sovereignty by looking at some other passages of Scripture.

God's Sovereignty throughout Scripture

Before we look more closely at some other important passages of Scripture, consider a section of the Bethlehem Baptist Church Elder Affirmation of Faith. Just as in so many other churches across the globe, the elders at Bethlehem have formally and joyously affirmed the doctrine of God's absolute sovereignty. They have chosen to express it in the following way.

> 3. 1 We believe that God, from all eternity, in order to display the full extent of his glory for the eternal and ever-increasing enjoyment of all who love him, did, by the most wise and holy counsel of his will, freely and unchangeably ordain and foreknow whatever comes to pass.

> 3. 2 We believe that God upholds and governs all things—from galaxies to subatomic particles, from the forces of nature to the movements of nations, and from the public plans of politicians to the secret acts of solitary persons—all in accord with his eternal, all-wise purposes to glorify himself, yet in such a way that he never sins, nor ever condemns a person unjustly; but that his ordaining and governing all things is compatible with the moral accountability of all persons created in his image.

3. 3 We believe that God's election is an uncondi-
tional act of free grace which was given through
his Son Christ Jesus before the world began. By
this act God chose, before the foundation of
the world, those who would be delivered from
bondage to sin and brought to repentance and
saving faith in his Son Christ Jesus.

Now, consider with me, first, the extent of support for this
in the Bible, and then some closing implications, and why
this doctrine is so precious.

The extent of God's sovereignty may be overwhelm-
ing for you. It is for me. And when we're confronted with
this truth we all face a choice. Will we turn from our
objections and praise his power and grace, bowing with
glad submission to the absolute sovereignty of God? Or
will we stiffen our neck and resist him? Will we see in the
sovereignty of God our only hope for life in our deadness;
our only hope for answers to our prayers; our only hope
for success in our evangelism; our only hope for meaning
in our suffering? Or will we insist that there is a better
hope—or no hope? That's the question we will face.

As paradoxical as it may seem to our finite minds,
nothing you are about to read below contradicts the real
moral responsibility of humans and angels and demons—
the responsibility to do what God commands. God has
given us a will. How we use it makes our eternal difference.

Let's divide God's sovereignty into his *governing of
natural events* and *his governing of human events*. In the first
case he is governing physical processes. In the second he is
governing human choices.

God's Sovereignty over Natural Events

God is sovereign over what appear to be the most random acts in the world. "The lot is cast into the lap, but its every decision is from the Lᴏʀᴅ" (Proverbs 16:33). In modern language we would say, "The dice are rolled on the table and every play is decided by God." There are no events so small that he does not rule each one for his purposes. "Are not two sparrows sold for a penny?", Jesus said, "and not one of them will fall to the ground apart from your Father. But even the hairs of your head are all numbered" (Matthew 10:29–30). Every roll of the dice in Las Vegas, every tiny bird that falls dead in the thousands of forests— all of this is by God's command.

From worms in the ground to stars in the galaxies, God governs the natural world. In the book of Jonah, God commands a fish to swallow a man (1:17), He commands a plant to grow (4:6), and a worm to kill that same plant (4:7). And far above the life of fish and plants and worms, the stars take their place and hold their place at God's command. "Lift up your eyes on high and see: who created these? He who brings out their host by number, calling them all by name; by the greatness of his might and because he is strong in power, not one is missing" (Isaiah 40:26). How much more, then, the natural events of this world— from weather to disasters to disease to disability to death.

> He sends out his command to the earth; his word runs swiftly. He gives snow like wool; he scatters frost like ashes. He hurls down his crystals of ice like crumbs; who can stand before his cold? He sends out his word, and melts them; he makes his wind blow and the waters flow. (Psalm 147:15–18)

> He loads the thick cloud with moisture; the
> clouds scatter his lightning. They turn around
> and around by his guidance, to accomplish all
> that he commands them on the face of the
> habitable world. Whether for correction or for
> his land or for love, he causes it to happen. (Job
> 37:11–13)

Snow and rain and cold and heat and wind are all the work of God. So when Jesus finds himself in the middle of a raging storm, he merely speaks, "'Peace! Be still!' And the wind ceased, and there was a great calm" (Mark 4:39). There is no wind, no storm, no hurricane, no cyclone, no typhoon, no monsoon, no tornado over which Jesus can say "Be still," and it will not obey. Which means, that if it blows, he intends for it to blow. "Does disaster come to a city, unless the LORD has done it?" (Amos 3:6). All Jesus had to do with any hurricane or tornado or natural disaster was say, "Be still," and there would have been no damage and no loss of life.

And what about the other sufferings of this life? "The LORD said to [Moses], 'Who has made man's mouth? Who makes him mute, or deaf, or seeing, or blind? Is it not I, the LORD?'" (Exodus 4:11). And Peter said to the suffering saints in Asia Minor, "Let those who suffer according to God's will entrust their souls to a faithful Creator while doing good" (1 Peter 4:19). "It is better to suffer for doing good, if that should be God's will, than for doing evil" (1 Peter 3:17).

Whether we suffer from disability, or from the evil of others, or from any other cause, God is the one who ultimately decides. The same is true of whether we live or die. Deuteronomy 32:39 says, "There is no god beside me; I kill and I make alive; I wound and I heal; and there is none that can deliver out of my hand." And the same is true of our daily doings. For James 4:13–15 reads,

> Come now, you who say, "Today or tomorrow we will go into such and such a town and spend a year there and trade and make a profit"—yet you do not know what tomorrow will bring. What is your life? For you are a mist that appears for a little time and then vanishes. Instead you ought to say, "If the Lord wills, we will live and do this or that."

Or as Job says, "Naked I came from my mother's womb, and naked shall I return. The LORD gave, and the LORD has taken away; blessed be the name of the LORD" (Job 1:21).

The roll of the dice, the fall of a bird, the crawl of a worm, the movement of stars, the falling of snow, the blowing of wind, the loss of sight, the suffering of saints, and the death of all, from the smallest to the greatest—these are included in the word of God: "I will accomplish all my purpose."

God's Sovereignty over Human Events

When we turn from the natural world to consider the world of human actions and human choice, God's sovereignty is still amazingly extensive. You should vote in political elections—on the candidates and the amendments and the budget matters and everything else. But let there be no man-exalting illusion that mere human beings will be the decisive cause in any victory or loss. God alone will have that supreme role. "He changes times and seasons; he removes kings and sets up kings.... the Most High rules the kingdom of men and gives it to whom he will" (Daniel 2:21; 4:17).

And whoever the President may be, that person is not sovereign. That person is being governed. And we should pray that our President would know that, "The king's heart is a stream of water in the hand of the Lord; he turns it wherever he will" (Proverbs 21:1). And when he engages in foreign affairs he will not be decisive, God will. "The LORD brings the counsel of the nations to nothing; he frustrates the plans of the peoples. The counsel of the LORD stands forever, the plans of his heart to all generations" (Psalm 33:10–11).

When nations came to do their absolute worst—the murder of the Son of God, Jesus Christ—they had not slipped out of God's control, but were doing his sweetest bidding at their worst moment: "Truly in this city there were gathered together against your holy servant Jesus, whom you anointed, both Herod and Pontius Pilate, along with the Gentiles and the peoples of Israel, to do *whatever your hand and your plan had predestined to take place*" (Acts 4:27–28).

The worst sin that ever happened was in God's plan. And by that sin, sin died. Our salvation was secured on Calvary under the sovereign hand of God. If you are a believer in Jesus, if you love him, you are a walking miracle. God granted you repentance (2 Timothy 2:25). God drew you to Christ (John 6:44). God revealed the Son of God to you (Matthew 11:27). God gave you the gift of faith. "By grace you have been saved through faith. And this is not your own doing; it is the gift of God, not a result of works, so that no one may boast" (Ephesians 2:8–9). The sovereignty of God in our salvation excludes boasting.

A hundred horrible things may have happened in your life. But if today you are moved to treasure Christ as your Lord and Savior, you can write over every one of those horrors the words of Genesis 50:20: Satan, "You meant evil against me, but God meant it for good."

Remember the words of Paul in Ephesians 1:11, God "works all things according to the counsel of his will." All things—from the roll of the dice, to the circuits of stars, to the rise of presidents, to the death of Jesus, to the gift of repentance and faith.

Seven Exhortations

What does God's sovereignty mean for our lives as believers? Why is this truth astonishing and unimaginably precious? I will state these reasons as exhortations.

Because God is sovereign…
1. Let us stand in awe of the sovereign authority and freedom and wisdom and power of God.
2. Let us never trifle with life as though it were a small or light affair.
3. Let us marvel at our own salvation—that God bought it and wrought it with sovereign power, and we are not our own.
4. Let us groan over the God-belittling man-centeredness of our culture and much of the church.
5. Let us be bold at the throne of grace, knowing that our prayers for the most difficult things can be answered. Nothing is too hard for God.

6. Let us rejoice that our evangelism will not be in vain, because there is no sinner so hard that the sovereign grace of God cannot break through.

7. Let us be thrilled and calm in these days of great upheaval because victory belongs to God, and no purposes that he wills to accomplish can be stopped.

More about the Sovereignty of God

THE PRECIOUSNESS OF GOD'S SOVEREIGNTY IN OUR PAIN

The deep inner workings of the Christian soul are not possible without the sovereignty of God. Why? Because the strength of hope and peace and joy and contentment and gladness and satisfaction and delight in God, which sustain the soul through sorrows and pain, are rooted in the confidence that God has the authority, the freedom, the wisdom, and the power to accomplish all the good he has promised to do for his embattled children.

No obstacle in nature, no obstacle from Satan, no obstacle in the failures and sins of man can stop God from making all my experiences, all my brokenness, and all my adversaries serve my eternal wholeness and joy. I hope you hear in that statement how my exuberance for God's sovereignty rests, not mainly on his causality in the past, but mainly on his powerful capacities in the future. The main reason God's sovereignty is precious is that he has power to fulfill "impossible" promises to me in my troubled or even seemingly hopeless condition. His rule over the past, including over the causes of my brokenness and pain, is simply a pre-condition of this hope-filled power. So let's take a very brief glimpse at this sovereignty.

Sovereign over Disability

As we saw earlier in this chapter, one of the most sweeping and foundational texts on the sovereignty of God deals directly with disabilities. In Exodus 4:11 God answers Moses's fear that his eloquence is insufficient for the task, "The LORD said to him, 'Who has made man's mouth? Who makes him mute, or deaf, or seeing, or blind? Is it not I, the LORD?'" Speech impediments, deafness, blindness—all disabilities are in God's hands to give and to remove. To this we may respond, "What about natural causes? What about Satan? What about the sins of others against us, or even our own sin?" And the answer is that these are real, but that none is finally decisive. If any of these play a role in our disability—and they do—they do so within God's sovereign plan.

For example, Romans 8:22–23 makes clear that our physical groaning over disease and disability is owing to the fact that our bodies share in the fall of all nature into futility. "We know that the whole creation has been groaning together in the pains of childbirth until now. And not only the creation, but we ourselves, who have the firstfruits of the Spirit, groan inwardly as we wait eagerly for adoption as sons, the redemption of our bodies."

So one cause of our physical and mental brokenness is that we share with the whole creation in its subjection to futility. But that creation is under the detailed governance of God. While there are natural causes for our disabilities, infirmities, diseases, and limitations, none of these natural causes is ultimate; none is finally decisive. God is.

Sovereign over Satan

So it is with Satan, as well. He is real. And he is involved in damaging and hurting God's people, including physically and mentally (Acts 10:38). But he is under God's governance. In the book of Job, Satan must come to God for permission to hurt Job (1:12; 2:6). And when Satan has done his work, striking Job with loathsome sores (2:7), Job says, "Shall we receive good *from God*, and shall we not receive evil?" (2:10). And the inspired author of the book says that Job was comforted "for all the evil that *the Lord had brought upon him*" (42:11).

So yes, Satan is real and no doubt has a hand in causing many diseases and disabilities. But he can do nothing without God's permission. And what God foreknows and permits, he plans. And what he plans for his children is always for their good.

Sovereign over Sin and Its Effects

And so it is with sins. We may smoke our way into emphysema, or we may lose a leg because a drunk driver crashes into us. But neither our sins nor the sins of another are finally decisive in what happens to us. God is. Again, the Christian may write over every attack of nature, Satan, or sin the words of Genesis 50:20, "As for you, you meant evil against me, but God meant it for good."

We can say this, even though we are undeserving sinners, because God said it first over all the sins that brought his Son to the cross for us. Herod, Pilate, cruel soldiers, shouting crowds—they meant the Son's execution for evil, but God meant it for good (Acts 4:27–28). That's the foundation of all the good that God promises in and through our suffering. And the good which God has in mind for his children has an immeasurable number of layers.

> *He means it for greater faith.* "We felt that we had received the sentence of death. But that was to make us rely not on ourselves but on God who raises the dead" (2 Corinthians 1:9).

> *He means it for greater righteousness.* "For the moment all discipline seems painful rather than pleasant, but later it yields the peaceful fruit of righteousness" (Hebrews 12:11).

> *He means it for greater hope.* "We rejoice in our sufferings, knowing that suffering produces endurance, and endurance produces character, and character produces hope" (Romans 5:3–4).

> *He means it for our greater experience of the glory of God.* "For this light momentary affliction is preparing for us an eternal weight of glory beyond all comparison" (2 Corinthians 4:17).

"*You*, Satan, *you*, natural causes, *you*, sinner—you all meant my suffering for evil, but God meant it for good—the good of greater faith, the good of greater righteousness, the good of greater hope, the good of greater glory." Or, as John 9:3 suggests, don't even consider secondary causes, because "It was not that this man sinned, or his parents, but that the works of God might be displayed in him."

Only God Is Decisive

Though nature and Satan and sin may have a hand in our suffering and pain, and should be resisted with prayer and truth and medicine or other appropriate means, nevertheless they are not decisive. God is. And thus we are left not with a theological problem about the past, but with an invincible hope for the future. If God is sovereign, then nothing is too hard for him. And by the blood of his Son he has promised infallibly...

> God will supply all your needs according to his riches in glory in Christ Jesus. (Philippians 4:19)

> His power will be made perfect in your weakness. (See 2 Corinthians 12:9)

> He will strengthen you and help you and uphold you with his righteous right hand. (See Isaiah 41:10)

> He will never leave you nor forsake you. (See Hebrews 13:5)

> He will not let any testing come upon you for which he does not give you grace to bear. (See 1 Corinthians 10:13)

> He will take the sting away from your death with the blood of his Son. (See 1 Corinthians 15:55-57)

> He will raise you from the dead, imperishable. (See 1 Corinthians 15:52)

> He will transform your lowly body to be like his glorious body, by the power that enables him even to subject all things to himself. (See Philippians 3:21)

And he will do this without fail because he is
absolutely sovereign over everything, and therefore he can do all things, and no purpose of his
can be thwarted. (See Job 42:2)

This is the foundation of our hope, and the key to the inner
workings of the Christian soul.

ROMANS 5:1–11

Therefore, since we have been justified by faith, we have peace with God through our Lord Jesus Christ. [2] Through him we have also obtained access by faith into this grace in which we stand, and we rejoice in hope of the glory of God. [3] Not only that, but we rejoice in our sufferings, knowing that suffering produces endurance, [4] and endurance produces character, and character produces hope, [5] and hope does not put us to shame, because God's love has been poured into our hearts through the Holy Spirit who has been given to us. [6] For while we were still weak, at the right time Christ died for the ungodly. [7] For one will scarcely die for a righteous person—though perhaps for a good person one would dare even to die— [8] but God shows his love for us in that while we were still sinners, Christ died for us. [9] Since, therefore, we have now been justified by his blood, much more shall we be saved by him from the wrath of God. [10] For if while we were enemies we were reconciled to God by the death of his Son, much more, now that we are reconciled, shall we be saved by his life. [11] More than that, we also rejoice in God through our Lord Jesus Christ, through whom we have now received reconciliation.

5

The Gospel of God in Christ

The men and women in Christian ministry I most admire have one trait in common (among others): they are all wary of deviating from the historic teachings of the church. The last thing any of us want is to promote new doctrines exclusive to us. We want to be arm-in-arm with millions of faithful followers of God's word. Truth does divide, but it also unites, and it is the uniting power of truth that we delight in most.

So those of us who teach have a special obligation to regularly test our interpretations of the Bible, in part by looking back into church history. If we can't find our interpretations represented there, we should be very slow to embrace them. Cults and sects are born in the minds of leaders who crave to be different. Jehovah's Witnesses, Mormons, the Unification Church, Christian Science—these were born in the minds of teachers who wanted new revelations and interpretations. They were restless with the limitations of the Bible and its historic understanding.

There is a lot of healthy and warranted warning these days about historical hero worship. Warnings about inordinate and uncritical admiration and imitation of historical teachers like Augustine, Aquinas, Calvin, Luther, the Puritans, Edwards, Wesley, Spurgeon, Barth, Chesterton, Lewis, etc. But we should be careful not to overdo this criticism. People with great historical heroes tend not to think of *themselves* as heroes. They're too busy learning from their heroes. Which means that, for all its dangers, admiring a great line of historical heroes will at least help keep you from starting a sect.

The ten truths set forth in this book are not new to Christianity. They're not distinctive or "niche" or exclusive or eccentric. They all have wide foundations in the Bible and deep roots in the history of God's people. And if any of them ever deserved to be guarded from the distortion of novelty, it is the ultimate electrically future-creating reality which is the subject of this chapter: the gospel of Jesus Christ.

The gospel is the good news that God in Christ paid the price of suffering, so that we could have the prize of enjoying him forever. Talk about turning the world upside down—God paid the price of his Son to give us the prize of himself! To put it another way, *God in Christ is the price and the prize of the gospel.*

That is my thesis for this chapter. To unfold its meaning and to show how biblical it is, I think it will be helpful to take three snapshots from three different places: one from Romans 5, one from church history, and one from 1 Corinthians 15.

The Price and Prize of the Gospel in Romans 5

Keep in mind that *gospel* means "good news"—in this case God's good news for the world. What is the price and the prize of that good news according to Romans 5? "While we were still weak, at the right time Christ died for the ungodly. 7 For one will scarcely die for a righteous person— though perhaps for a good person one would dare even to die— 8 but God shows his love for us in that while we were still sinners, Christ died for us" (Romans 5:6–8).

The *price* of the gospel is the death of Christ: "Christ died for the ungodly" (v. 6). That is, "Christ died for us" (v. 8). God loved us while we were sinners and paid a price so that we might have an infinite prize. That price was the death of his Son. And what was the prize that he bought for us when he paid that price?

> Since, therefore, we have now been justified by his blood, much more shall we be saved by him from the wrath of God. 10 For if while we were enemies we were reconciled to God by the death of his Son, much more, now that we are reconciled, shall we be saved by his life. 11 More than that, we also rejoice in God through our Lord Jesus Christ, through whom we have now received reconciliation. (Romans 5:9–11)

The prize God purchased for us by the price of his Son is this: "we have now been *justified* by his blood." And "much more," because of that justification we will be saved by him from wrath—the wrath of God (v. 9) But is that the highest, best, fullest, most satisfying prize of the gospel?

Note that verse 10 contains a second "much more," that we shall "be saved by his life." And verse 11 takes it up yet another level, "*More* than that: we rejoice in God." That is the final and highest good of the good news. There is not another "more" after that. There is only Paul's saying again in verse 11 how we got there: we "rejoice in God through our Lord Jesus Christ, through whom we have now received reconciliation."

So the end of the gospel is that we "rejoice in God." The highest, fullest, deepest, sweetest good of the gospel is God himself, enjoyed by his redeemed people. Hence the thesis, *God in Christ is the price and the prize of the gospel.* God in Christ became the price (Romans 5:6–8), and God in Christ became the prize (Romans 5:11). The gospel is the good news that God bought for us the everlasting enjoyment of God. That's what I mean when I say, "God is the gospel."

For five hundred years, Protestant Christians have summed up the gospel in terms of the five "solas," Latin for *only* or *alone.* And all I'm doing in giving you this summary is adding one that is implicit in the others. So in these historical forms I would define the gospel like this:

> As revealed with final authority in Scripture alone
> the Gospel is the good news that
> by faith alone
> through grace alone
> on the basis of Christ alone
> for the glory of God alone
> sinners have full and final joy in God alone.

All these affirmations are grounded in the Bible.

Scripture alone is the final authority for revealing

and defining the gospel of Christ. "If anyone is preaching to you a gospel contrary to the one you received, let him be accursed" (Galatians 1:9). The apostolic delivery of the gospel is final and decisive.

By *faith alone*. "We hold that one is justified by faith apart from works of the law" (Romans 3:28). Faith plus nothing is the way we receive the gift of justification.

Through *grace alone*. "When we were dead in our trespasses, [God] made us alive together with Christ—by *grace* you have been saved—… For by *grace* you have been saved through faith. And this is not your own doing; it is the gift of God, not a result of works, so that no one may boast" (Ephesians 2:5, 8–9).

On the basis of *Christ alone*. Christ "has no need, like those high priests, to offer sacrifices daily, first for his own sins and then for those of the people, since he did this once for all when he offered up himself" (Hebrews 7:27; see also 9:12; 10:10.) *Once for all* and decisively. Nothing can be added to the work of Christ to cover our sins, and that work cannot be repeated.

For *the glory of God alone*. God "predestined us for adoption as sons through Jesus Christ… to the praise of his glorious grace" (Ephesians 1:5–6). God saved us in such a way that there would be no human boasting (Ephesians 2:9; 1 Corinthians 1:26–31), but all would show his glory.

Full and final joy in *God alone*. "In your presence
there is fullness of joy; at your right hand are
pleasures forevermore" (Psalm 16:11). "Whom
have I in heaven but you? And there is nothing
on earth that I desire besides you. My flesh and
my heart may fail, but God is the strength of my
heart and my portion forever" (Psalm 73:25–26).

This is the gospel as millions of Christians have thought
about it for centuries, and we should be happy to link arms
with this great Reformation heritage: God in Christ *is* the
price and the prize of the gospel.

The Price and Prize of the Gospel in 1 Corinthians 15

There are six important elements in 1 Corinthians 15, five of
which are explicit in the text and one of which is implicit.

Now I would remind you, brothers, of the gospel
I preached to you, which you received, in which
you stand, ² and by which you are being saved, if
you hold fast to the word I preached to you—
unless you believed in vain. ³ For I delivered to
you as of first importance what I also received:
that Christ died for our sins in accordance with
the Scriptures, ⁴ that he was buried, that he was
raised on the third day in accordance with the
Scriptures. (1 Corinthians 15:1–4)

Here we see six elements of the gospel. If any of these six
were missing, there would be no gospel.

The Gospel Is a Divine Plan

"Christ died for our sins *in accordance with the Scriptures*" (v. 3b). That is, in accordance with the Scriptures written hundreds of years before he died. Which means the gospel was planned by God long before it took place.

The Gospel Is a Historical Event

"Christ died" (v. 3b). The gospel is not mythology. It is not mere ideas or feelings. It is an event. And without the event there is no gospel.

The Gospel Is the Divine Achievements Accomplished through That Event

That is, through that death—things God accomplished in the death of Jesus long before we ever existed. "Christ died *for our sins*" (v. 3b). "For our sins" means this death had design in it. It was meant to accomplish something. It accomplished the canceling of the record of debt against us (Colossians 2:14), the removal of God's wrath (Romans 5:9) and of the curse of the law (Galatians 3:13), the condemnation of sin (Romans 8:3), and the purchase of eternal life (John 3:16). These are objective achievements of the work of Christ, before they are applied to anyone.

The Gospel Is a Free Offer of Christ for Faith

"The gospel I preached to you, which you received, in which you stand, and by which you are being saved, if you hold fast to the word I preached to you—unless you *believed* in vain" (1 Corinthians 15: 1–2). The good news of God's achievements in Christ become ours by faith, by believing, by receiving. Not by deserving or working or giving a performance. What God has done is free to all who will have it. It is received by faith. Without the free offer of Christ for faith there would be no gospel.

The Gospel Is an Application to Individual Believers of What God Objectively Achieved in the Death of Jesus

So when we believe, then we are forgiven for our sins (Acts 10:43), we are justified (Romans 5:1), and we receive eternal life (John 3:16), along with dozens of other benefits. (To catalog those benefits I wrote the book, *Fifty Reasons Why Jesus Came to Die*). The gospel is the powerful, personal application to us of what God achieved for us on the cross.

The Gospel Is the Enjoyment of Fellowship with God Himself

This is implicit in the word *gospel* ("good news"). If you ask, "What is the highest, deepest, most satisfying, all-encompassing good of the good news?" The answer is: God himself known and enjoyed by his redeemed people. This is made explicit in 1 Peter 3:18, "Christ also suffered once for sins, the righteous for the unrighteous, *that he might bring us to God.*" All the other gifts of the gospel exist to make this one possible. We are forgiven so that our guilt does not keep us away from God. We are justified so that our condemnation does not keep us away from God. We are given eternal life now, with new bodies in the resurrection, so that we have the capacities for enjoying God to the fullest. Test your heart. Why do you want forgiveness? Why do you want to be justified? Why do you want eternal life? Is the decisive answer, "Because I want to enjoy God"?

In summary then, *God in Christ is the price and the prize of the gospel.* The prize of the gospel is the Person who paid the price. The gospel-love God gives is ultimately the gift of himself. This is what we were made for. This is what we lost in our sin. This is what Christ came to restore. "In your presence there is fullness of joy; at your right hand are pleasures forevermore" (Psalm 16:11).

The Love of God Is the Gift of Himself

I offer the following quote to you on behalf of Christ. Indeed, I urge you to receive it. It's free. See in this the beauty of Christ and receive him as your Treasure and your Lord and your Savior, for this is what it means to believe the gospel. This is the most beautiful description I have ever read of what I mean by "God is the gospel" and "The love of God is the gift of himself." It comes from Jonathan Edwards in 1731, when he was 28.

> The redeemed have all their objective good in God. God himself is the great good which they are brought to the possession and enjoyment of by redemption. He is the highest good, and the sum of all that good which Christ purchased.
>
> God is the inheritance of the saints; he is the portion of their souls. God is their wealth and treasure, their food, their life, their dwelling place, their ornament and diadem, and their everlasting honor and glory. They have none in heaven but God; he is the great good which the redeemed are received to at death, and which they are to rise to at the end of the world. The Lord God, he is the light of the heavenly Jerusalem; and is the "river of the water of life" that runs, and the tree of life that grows, "in the midst of the paradise of God."

The glorious excellencies and beauty of God will
be what will forever entertain the minds of the
saints, and the love of God will be their everlasting feast. The redeemed will indeed enjoy other
things; they will enjoy the angels, and will enjoy
one another: but that which they shall enjoy
in the angels, or each other, or in anything else
whatsoever, that will yield them delight and happiness, will be what will be seen of God in them.

> (Jonathan Edwards, "God Glorified in the Work
> of Redemption, by the Greatness of Man's Depen-
> dence upon Him, in the Whole of It [1731]" {sermon
> on 1 Corinthians 1:29–31} in: Wilson H. Kimnach,
> Kenneth P. Minkema, and Douglas A. Sweeney, ed.,
> *The Sermons of Jonathan Edwards: A Reader* [New
> Haven: Yale University Press, 1999], 74–75.)

Amen.

More about the Gospel

HOW IS THE GOSPEL THE POWER OF GOD UNTO SALVATION?

Let's dwell on the words of Romans 1:16, "For [the
gospel] is the power of God for salvation to everyone who
believes."

I will take up only one question: *What is this salvation
that the gospel so powerfully brings about?* By answering this
question, we will see how our faith relates to the gospel in
bringing about our salvation.

"The gospel…is the power of God for salvation"
(Romans 1:16). Does this mean, "The gospel is the power

of God to win converts"? I do think that is true, but I don't
think that is what *this* statement means.

I think it is true that the gospel converts people—
brings them to faith and repentance—because Romans
10:17 says, "So faith *comes* from hearing, and hearing
through the word of Christ." Moreover, 1 Peter 1:23–25
says, "You have been born again, not of perishable seed but
of imperishable, through the living and abiding word of
God.... And this word is the good news that was preached
to you." So it is true that we are born of God and converted by means of hearing the powerful word of God, the
gospel.

And it's true that this conversion is called "salvation"
in the New Testament. For example Paul says, "For by
grace you have been *saved* through faith. And this is not
your own doing; it is the gift of God, not a result of works,
so that no one may boast" (Ephesians 2:8–9). So conversion to Christ by faith is called "being saved." If you are
a believer in Christ, you "have been saved." The Book of
Romans should be precious beyond words to you, because,
like no other book in the Bible, it unfolds for you what has
already happened in God's saving you—your election, your
predestination, your calling, your justification, your sanctification, and the obedience of faith. These are all part of
the salvation that is already true of you through faith.

But what is the salvation that Paul has in mind in
Romans 1:16? What does he mean when he says, "For [the
gospel] is the power of God for salvation to everyone who
believes"? I think he has in mind not primarily the first
event of conversion, but primarily *the final triumph of the
gospel in bringing believers to eternal safety and joy in the
presence of a holy and glorious God.*

There are four reasons why I think this is what he means. Looking at these reasons is the best way to unpack the meaning of the verse.

The Power of the Gospel Is What Frees Us from Being Ashamed of the Gospel

"I am not ashamed of the gospel, for it is the power of God for salvation" (Romans 1:16). If this meant only that the gospel has the power to make converts, why would that solve the shame problem? Lots of religions produce a kind of conversion. Lots of different religious and secular movements win people over to their faith. When Paul said that the gospel has such a powerful effect that you don't have to be ashamed of it, did he simply mean that it does what other religions do? Is it that the gospel simply wins converts? I don't think so.

Jesus triumphed over shame by looking at the future joy that was set before him as he died. I think this is what Paul, as well, has in mind in Romans 1:16. You don't have to be ashamed of the gospel because it doesn't just make converts; *it saves those converts utterly*. It brings them to final safety and ever-increasing joy in the presence of a glorious and holy God forever and ever. This is what makes us bold with the gospel—not that it can make converts (any religion can do that)—but that it is the only truth in the world that can really save people forever and bring them to everlasting joy with God.

Elsewhere in Paul and the New Testament, the Word Salvation Is Future-Oriented

The second reason I think "salvation" in verse 16 refers to *the final triumph of the gospel in bringing believers to eternal safety and joy in the presence of a holy and glorious God* is that the phrase "for [unto] salvation" has this future-oriented meaning elsewhere in Paul and other New Testament writers.

For example, in 2 Thessalonians 2:13 Paul says, "God chose you as the firstfruits to be saved, through sanctification by the Spirit and belief in the truth." Now here, salvation is not just what happens at conversion, which leads to sanctification, but salvation is what comes later, in the future, "*through* sanctification." In other words, in this verse "salvation" refers to the future triumph that brings the saint into God's presence with everlasting joy.

Or again, in 2 Corinthians 7:10, Paul speaks to Christians who are already converted and saved, but need fresh repentance for their sins: "For godly grief produces a repentance that leads to salvation without regret, whereas worldly grief produces death." Here again, "to salvation" refers not to conversion, but to the final, future state of safety and joy in the presence of God. (See also 2 Timothy 3:15.)

Similarly, Hebrews 9:28 says, "Christ... will appear a second time, not to deal with sin but to save those who are eagerly waiting for him." This final, complete salvation happens at the Second Coming. First Peter 1:5 says that believers "by God's power are being guarded through faith for a salvation ready to be revealed in the last time." This is not conversion. It is the last great work of God—"ready to be revealed in the last time"—to rescue us and bring us to safety and joy in his presence forever.

Paul talks about this future salvation as rescue from the final wrath of God.

Since, therefore, we have now been justified by

> his blood, [that's the present reality of salvation!]
> much more shall we be saved by him from the
> wrath of God. For if while we were enemies we
> were reconciled to God by the death of his Son
> [here again is the present reality of salvation!],
> much more, now that we are reconciled, shall we
> be saved by his life. (Romans 5:9–10)

The full experience of salvation, in Paul's thinking, is still
future. Thus he says, "Salvation is nearer to us now than
when we first believed" (Romans 13:11).

So when Paul says in Romans 1:16 that "the gospel…
is the power of God for salvation," I take him to mean that
the gospel is the only message in the world that can bring
a person not just to conversion, but to everlasting safety
and joy in the presence of a holy and glorious God.

Ongoing Belief Is the Condition for This Salvation

The third reason I think "salvation" in Romans 1:16 is *the
final triumph of the gospel in bringing believers to eternal
safety and joy in the presence of a holy and glorious God* is that
ongoing belief is the condition for this salvation.

Notice that verse 16 does not say that the gospel "is
the power of God to bring about faith and salvation." It
says that the gospel "is the power of God for [unto] salvation to everyone who believes [present tense in Greek, "is
believing," signifying continuous action]." Paul's point here
is not that the power of the gospel creates faith, but that,
for those who have faith, the gospel brings about salvation.
So the point in this passage is not that the gospel is the
power for conversion *to* faith; the point is that the gospel
is the power to bring about future, final salvation *through* a
life of faith.

The tense of the verb "believe" here is crucial. It signifies ongoing action, not just the first act of faith when you were converted: "The gospel … is the power of God for salvation to everyone who [*is believing*]"—those who go on believing. It's the same as 1 Corinthians 15:1–2 where Paul says, "I preached to you [the gospel], which you received, in which you stand, and by which you are being saved, *if you hold fast to the word which I preached to you—unless you believed in vain*." Faith that does not persevere is a vain and empty faith—what James calls dead faith (James 2:17, 26).

So the point of Romans 1:16 is that you don't have to be ashamed of the gospel *because* it is the only truth in the world which, if you go on banking on it day after day, will triumph over every obstacle and bring you to eternal safety and joy in the presence of a holy and glorious God.

Paul Says the Gospel Is for Believers, Not Just Unbelievers

The last reason I think "salvation" in Romans 1:16 is *the final triumph of the gospel in bringing believers to eternal safety and joy in the presence of a holy and glorious God* is that the verse is given as the reason Paul wants to preach the gospel to believers (not just unbelievers).

We've seen this already, but look again. In verse 15 Paul says, "I am eager to preach the gospel to you also who are in Rome." He is eager to preach the gospel to "you"— you believers, not just unbelievers. Then he gives the reason: because he is not ashamed of it, because it is the power of God for salvation to all such believers.

So I conclude that the reason Paul is not ashamed of the gospel is that it is the only truth in all the world that will not let you down when you give your life to it in faith.

It will bring you all the way through temptation and persecution and death and judgment, into eternal safety and
ever-increasing joy in the presence of a holy and glorious
God. All the other "gospels" in the world that win so many
converts will fail you in the end. Only one gospel saves
from the final wrath of God and leads to fullness of joy in
his presence and pleasures at his right hand forever. Therefore, there is no need to be ashamed of it, no matter what
others say or do. And oh how eager we should be to speak
this gospel to believer and unbeliever alike!

Do you feed your faith day by day with the promises of this triumphant gospel? Do you, as a believer, go
to the gospel day by day and savor its power in verses
like Romans 8:32, "He who did not spare his own Son
but gave him up for us all, how will he not also with him
graciously give us all things?" The gospel is the good news
that God gave us his Son, so as to obtain for us everything
that would be good for us. Therefore, the gospel is the
power that gives us victory over temptation to despair and
to pride and to greed and to lust. The gospel alone can
triumph over every obstacle and bring us to eternal joy.
Whatever it costs you, stand in it, hold it fast, believe on
it, feed on it, savor it, count it more precious than silver or
gold. The gospel will save you. And it alone.

> I love to tell the story; for those who know it
> best seem hungering and thirsting to hear it, like
> the rest. And when, in scenes of glory, I sing the
> new, new song, 'twill be the old, old story that I
> have loved so long.

> I love to tell the story,
> 'twill be my theme in glory

To tell the old, old story
Of Jesus and his love. (Katherine Hankey
[1834–1911], "Tell Me the Old, Old Story")

MATTHEW 28:16–20

Now the eleven disciples went to Galilee, to the mountain to which Jesus had directed them. [17] And when they saw him they worshiped him, but some doubted. [18] And Jesus came and said to them, "All authority in heaven and on earth has been given to me. [19] Go therefore and make disciples of all nations, baptizing them in the name of the Father and of the Son and of the Holy Spirit, [20] teaching them to observe all that I have commanded you. And behold, I am with you always, to the end of the age."

6
The Call to Global Missions

In 1890, Bethlehem Baptist Church—at that time a 29-year-old Swedish Baptist Church—sent members Mini and Ola Hanson to an unreached people group in Burma called the Kachin. These people were known as vengeful, cruel, and treacherous. The King of Burma declared to the Hansons when they got there, "So you are to teach the Kachins! Do you see my dogs over there? I tell you, it will be easier to convert and teach these dogs. You are wasting your life."

The Kachin were completely illiterate, with no written language. Over the next 30 years, Ola Hanson identified and documented 25,000 of their words and published a Kachin-English dictionary. In 1911, he finished translating the New Testament into Kachin. On August 11, 1926 he completed the Old Testament.

In a letter dated August 14 of that year, Hanson wrote, "It is with heartfelt gratitude that I lay this work at the feet of my Master. Pray with us, that our divine Master may bless this work to the salvation of the whole Kachin race." Today virtually all Kachin can read and write in their own language, as well as Burmese, the national language. And there are more than half a million Kachin Christians.

It has been one of the highest privileges of my life to be part of the effort to sustain and grow the legacy of missions at Bethlehem Baptist Church, a legacy at this point nearly 130 years in the making. While pastoring there I often thought: *O Lord, if we falter as a church, if we stumble, if we drop the ropes, so many missionaries will fall.* For we had hundreds of global partners who had gone down into the mines on ropes held by the church (this is still true at Bethlehem today).

"Holding the rope" has long been a powerful image for missions work. It comes from William Carey, who blazed the trail to India in 1792 and saw his mission as that of a miner penetrating into a deep mine—one which had never been explored, and with no one to guide. He said to Andrew Fuller and John Ryland and his other pastor friends, "I will go down, if you will hold the rope." And John Ryland reports, "He took an oath from each of us, at the mouth of the pit, to this effect: that 'while we lived, we should never let go of the rope.'" (Peter Morden, *Offering Christ to the World* [Waynesboro, Georgia: Paternoster, 2003], 167.)

We are, all of us who believe, either goers, senders, or disobedient—those who drop into mines, those who hold the ropes, or those who think it's not their business. Rejoice if you are part of a church that doesn't just *support*, but *sends* from your own number, families and singles, to take the gospel to the peoples of the world.

Ten Biblical Convictions Regarding Global Missions

Here are ten biblical convictions that have long driven my commitment to world missions. I pray that they will burn in your soul—for some of you as a God-given compulsion to go, and for others as a God-given compulsion to send.

God Is Passionately Committed to the Fame of His Name, and That He Be Worshiped by All the Peoples of the World— And This Is Not Egomania, It Is Love

Missions, global outreach, is about joining God in his passion to love the nations by offering himself to them for the overflowing joy of their praise.

> Declare his glory among the nations, his marvelous works among all the peoples! (Psalm 96:3).

> Make known his deeds among the peoples, proclaim that his name is exalted (Isaiah 12:4).

> God sends Jesus on his mission, "in order that the Gentiles might glorify God for his mercy" (Romans 15:9).

> He does his mighty works in history, "that [his] name might be proclaimed in all the earth" (Romans 9:17).

Therefore, Worship Is the Goal and the Fuel of Missions; Missions Exists Because Worship Doesn't

Missions is a way of saying that *the joy of knowing Christ is not a private or tribal or national or ethnic privilege. It is for all.* And that's why Christians go. Because we have tasted the joy of worshiping Jesus, and we want all the families of the earth included. "All the ends of the earth shall remember and turn to the LORD, and all the families of the nations shall worship before you" (Psalm 22:27).

Seeking the worship of the nations is fueled by the joy of our own worship. You can't commend what you don't cherish. You can't proclaim what you don't prize. Worship is the fuel and the goal of missions.

People Must Be Told about Jesus, Because There Is No Salvation and No Worship Where the Gospel of the Crucified and Risen Son of God Is Not Heard and Believed

There will be no salvation and no true worship among people who have not heard the gospel. Missions is essential for salvation.

> And there is salvation in no one else, for there is no other name under heaven given among men by which we must be saved. (Acts 4:12)

> Faith comes from hearing, and hearing through the word of Christ. (Romans 10:17)

> Whoever has the Son has life; whoever does not have the Son of God does not have life. (1 John 5:12)

> Go therefore and make disciples of all nations. (Matthew 28:19)

God Is Committed to Gathering Worshipers from All the Peoples of the World, Not Just All the Countries of the World

This is what "all nations" means in the Great Commission. Nations like Ojibwe and Fulani and Kachin, not like the United States and Japan and Argentina. This is what Jesus bought with his blood.

> Worthy are you to take the scroll and to open its seals, for you were slain, and by your blood you ransomed people for God from every tribe and language and people and nation, and you have made them a kingdom and priests to our God, and they shall reign on the earth. (Revelation 5:9–10)

The gospel has already reached all the *countries*. But, according to the Joshua Project (www.joshuaproject.net) there are more than 7,000 "unreached" or "minimally reached" *peoples*. That is why Bethlehem's mission statement says, "We exist to spread a passion for the supremacy of God in all things for the joy of all peoples [plural!] through Jesus Christ."

Therefore, There Is a Critical Need for Paul-Type Missionaries Whose Calling and Passion Is to Take the Gospel to Peoples Where There Is No Access to the Gospel at All

I am distinguishing Paul-type missionaries from Timothy-type missionaries. Timothy left his home and served cross culturally in a city (Ephesus) different from his own (Lystra). But Paul said in Romans 15:20, "I make it my ambition to preach the gospel, not where Christ has already been named." There is still much to do where Christ has been named. But oh how badly we need to pray for an army of hundreds of thousands with Paul's passion to reach the utterly unreached and unengaged peoples of the world.

We Must Send Global Partners in a Manner Worthy of God

This is why churches have a missions staff and a missions budget and a missions nurture program and support teams for missionaries. "You will do well to send them on their journey in a manner worthy of God" (3 John 6). This is why senders are crucial, along with goers, because not everyone is a frontier missionary. Frontier missionaries cross cultures and plant the church where it's not. But if we are not a goer, there is a great calling: that of sender. And John says we are to do it in a manner worthy of God.

It Is Fitting for Us to Have a Wartime Mindset in the Use of Our Resources as Long as Peoples Are without the Gospel and We Have Resources to Send It

In peacetime the Queen Mary was a luxury liner, but in the Second World War she became a troop carrier. Instead of bunks three-high they were stacked seven-high. Instead of 18-piece place settings, there were rations with fork and knife. You allocate your resources differently if it's wartime. And it *is* wartime. The battles are more constant than in any of our military conflicts, and the losses are eternal.

The Macedonians about whom Paul wrote are a model for us in the face of great need. "In a severe test of affliction, their abundance of joy and their extreme poverty have overflowed in a wealth of generosity on their part" (2 Corinthians 8:2). Oh, that we would deepen in our grasp of the urgency of the hour and remember that ultimately we don't own anything. God owns us and all we have. And he cares about how it goes with us, in our war effort to reach the nations with the gospel, the gospel that Jesus died to send.

Prayer Is a Wartime Walkie-Talkie, Not a Domestic Intercom

"I chose you and appointed you," Jesus said, "that you should go and bear fruit... *so that* whatever you ask the Father in my name, he may give it to you" (John 15:16). God has given you a wartime mission, to go and bear fruit.

And he gave you prayer for the purpose of accomplishing *that* mission.

One of the reasons our prayer malfunctions is that we try to treat it like a domestic intercom for calling the butler when we want another pillow in the den. But prayer is mainly for those on the front lines of the war effort, so they can call in to headquarters to send help. We are to treat prayer like a battlefield walkie-talkie for calling down the power of the Holy Spirit in the struggle for souls.

Suffering Is Not Only the Price for Being in Missions; It Is God's Plan for Getting the Job Done

This is not just the price many must pay. This is God's strategy for victory.

> If they have called the master of the house Beelzebul, how much more will they malign those of his household. (Matthew 10:25)

> They will deliver you up to tribulation and put you to death, and you will be hated by all nations for my name's sake. (Matthew 24:9)

> Behold, I am sending you out as sheep in the midst of wolves. (Matthew 10:16)

God's Son won the victory this way. So will we. "They have conquered him by the blood of the Lamb and by the word of their testimony, for they loved not their lives even unto death" (Revelation 12:11). They conquered (not "were conquered") by testimony and death.

The Global Cause of Christ Cannot Fail, and Nothing You Do in This Cause Is in Vain

Jesus said, "All authority in heaven and on earth has been

given to me. Go therefore and make disciples." (Matthew 28:18–19). Not some authority—all. He cannot be defeated. "I will build my church, and the gates of hell shall not prevail against it" (Matthew 16:18). "This gospel of the kingdom will be proclaimed throughout the whole world as a testimony to all nations, and then the end will come" (Matthew 24:14). He has ransomed a people for all the nations. And he will have them.

There are more, but these are ten of the main biblical convictions that can powerfully drive a commitment to global outreach. And for some of you, I pray that as you have been reading these convictions have become, again, a confirmation that God is leading you into long-term, cross-cultural missions.

More about the Call to Global Missions

FOUR MOTIVES FOR MISSIONS FROM JOHN 10:16

> *And I have other sheep that are not of this fold. I must bring them also, and they will listen to my voice. So there will be one flock, one shepherd.*
> *—John 10:16*

There are four things in John 10:16 that should fill us to overflowing with confidence in our missions-related dreaming and planning and labor.

Jesus Has Other Sheep
Christ has people besides those already converted—other

people besides us. "I have other sheep that are not of this fold." There will always be people who argue that the doctrine of predestination makes missions unnecessary. But they are wrong. It does not make missions unnecessary; it makes missions hopeful. John Alexander, a former president of Inter-Varsity, said in a message at Urbana '67, "At the beginning of my missionary career I said that if predestination were true, I could not be a missionary. Now after 20 years of struggling with the hardness of the human heart, I say I could never be a missionary unless I believed in the doctrine of predestination." It gives hope that Christ most certainly has a people among the nations. "I have other sheep."

It was precisely this truth that encouraged the apostle Paul when he was downcast in Corinth. "And the Lord said to Paul one night in a vision, 'Do not be afraid, but go on speaking and do not be silent, for I am with you, and no one will attack you to harm you, for I have many in this city who are my people.'" (Acts 18:9–10).

"I have other sheep that are not of this fold." It is a promise full of hope for those who dream about new fields of missionary labor.

These Sheep Are Scattered Outside the Present Fold

The verse implies that the "other sheep" that Christ has are scattered outside the present fold. This is made explicit where John explains a word of prophecy spoken by Caiaphas, the high priest: "He did not say this of his own accord, but being high priest that year he prophesied that Jesus should die for the nation, and not for the nation only, but to gather into one the children of God who are scattered abroad" (John 11:51–52).

Evangelism for the apostle John is the ingathering of the children of God. Of course, in John 1:12–13 it says that we become children of God by being born again and receiving Christ. This doesn't have to be a contradiction. John 11:52 simply means that God has already predestined who will be delivered from their slavery to sin and unbelief and become children of God by faith, so he calls these chosen ones "children of God" because from the divine perspective they are certainly going to be reached and saved.

But the point for our encouragement in missionary strategy is that they are *scattered*. They are not all pocketed in one or two places. They are scattered everywhere.

The way John put it when he wrote the Book of Revelation was, "for you were slain, and by your blood you ransomed people for God from every tribe and language and people and nation" (Revelation 5:9).

The ransomed children of God will be found in every people reached by the gospel. And that is a great encouragement to us, an encouragement to get on with the task of frontier missions in order to reach the hidden peoples.

The Lord Is Committed to His Lost Sheep

The Lord has committed himself to bring his lost sheep home. He will do it. "I have other sheep that are not of this fold; I must bring them also." *He* will bring them.

This does not mean, as some of the hyper-Calvinists thought it did in Carey's day, that Christ will gather in his sheep without asking us to participate! In John 20:21 Jesus says, "As the Father has sent me, even so I am sending you" (also see John 17:18). We continue the mission of Christ. So Jesus prays in 17:20, "I do not ask for these [his disciples] only, but also for those who will believe in me through their word."

In other words, just as the voice of the shepherd called his sheep from Jesus's own lips in Palestine, so he still speaks today through the gospel and calls his sheep by name, and they hear his voice and follow him. He does it. But not without us!

This is the wonder of the gospel. When it is preached truthfully in the power of the Spirit, it is not merely the word of man. It is the word of God (1 Thessalonians 2:13).

And in the presentation of the gospel, John 10:27 is just as true now as it was in Jesus's day: "My sheep hear *my* voice, and I know them, and they follow me." It is Christ who calls in the gospel. Christ gathers. We are only witnesses. That is why Paul said, "I will not venture to speak of anything except what Christ has accomplished through me bring the Gentiles to obedience" (Romans 15:18).

So we can take heart. All authority in heaven and on earth has been given to the Son of God and he declares that he must bring in his other sheep. He will do it.

The Sheep Will Come

This implies the final word of hope from John 10:16. *If he brings them, they will come*! "I have other sheep that are not of this fold; I must bring them also, and *they will listen to my voice*." None of Christ's sheep finally reject his word. What else can keep you going in a hard and unresponsive place of ministry, except that God reigns and those whom the Father has chosen will heed the voice of the Son?

Consider the story of Peter Cameron Scott, who was born in 1867 and founded the African Inland Mission. He had tried twice to serve in Africa but had to come home

both times with malaria. The third attempt was especially
joyful because he was joined by his brother John. But the
joy evaporated as John fell victim to the fever. Scott buried
his brother all by himself, and at the grave rededicated
himself to preach the gospel. But again his health broke
and he had to return to England, utterly discouraged.

In London, something wonderful happened. We read
about it in Ruth Tucker's, *From Jerusalem to Irian Jaya*.
Scott needed a fresh source of inspiration, and he found
it at a tomb in Westminster Abbey. In that tomb lay the
remains of a man who had inspired so many others in their
missionary service to Africa: David Livingstone. The spirit
of Livingstone seemed to be prodding Scott onward as he
knelt reverently and read the inscription,

> *Other sheep I have which are not of this fold; them
> also I must bring.*

Scott would return to Africa and lay down his life, if need
be, for the cause for which this great man had lived and
died.

> Lord, put a thorn in our cushion and courage in
> our hearts. And send us with joy and confidence
> to the unreached peoples of the earth. Give us a
> passion to be your instruments for the ingather-
> ing of the elect through all the world. Amen.

2 THESSALONIANS 1:3-5, 11-12

We ought always to give thanks to God for you, brothers, as is right, because your faith is growing abundantly, and the love of every one of you for one another is increasing. ⁴ Therefore we ourselves boast about you in the churches of God for your steadfastness and faith in all your persecutions and in the afflictions that you are enduring. ⁵ This is evidence of the righteous judgment of God, that you may be considered worthy of the kingdom of God, for which you are also suffering.... ¹¹ To this end we always pray for you, that our God may make you worthy of his calling and may fulfill every resolve for good and every work of faith by his power, ¹² so that the name of our Lord Jesus may be glorified in you, and you in him, according to the grace of our God and the Lord Jesus Christ.

7

Living the Christian Life

I first preached on this text at Bethlehem Baptist Church on the last Sunday of 1985. Little did I know that, in verses 11 and 12, I was uncovering for myself and for our church the foundations of what would become one of the most practical and important theological trademarks of that church: living by faith in future grace. Let me summarize these two verses, and then flesh out what it means to live by faith in future grace and how this becomes a conduit of God's power into your life.

Eight Crucial Things to See in 2 Thessalonians 1:11–12

There are eight absolutely crucial things to see in Paul's prayer. Here are verses 11 and 12 with those eight elements emphasized, and numbered in the order I address them below:

To this end we always pray for you, that our God
may [make you worthy (2)] of [his calling (1)]
and may [fulfill every resolve for good (3)] and
every [work of faith (5)] [by his power (4)], so
that [the name of our Lord Jesus may be glorified (6)] in you, [and you in him (7)], [according
to the grace of our God and the Lord Jesus
Christ (8)].

1. The Calling of God

"That our God may make you worthy of *his calling*." This
calling is our glorious destiny in God's kingdom and glory.
That's what Paul says in 1 Thessalonians 2:12, that he and
his fellow missionaries "charged you to walk in a manner
worthy of God, who calls you into his own kingdom and
glory." Your calling is to be in the kingdom of God and to
share the glory of God, as we will see in just a moment.

2. Being Made Worthy

"That our God may *make you worthy* of his calling." Being
made worthy doesn't mean being made deserving. It
means being made *suitable* or *fitting* or *appropriate* because
of the worth of another. So we might say, "I need to fix up
this room because the Queen of England is going to stay
with us and the room needs to be worthy of her dignity."
It needs to be fitting, suitable, appropriate. She didn't
decide to come because the room is inherently beautiful.
The room should be made beautiful because she's coming.
So we are being made suitable for our calling into God's
kingdom and glory.

3. Fulfillment of Good Resolves

"That our God may make you worthy of his calling and *may fulfill every resolve for good.*" The Christian life is a resolving, planning, purposing, intending life. We have minds and wills, and God expects that we will use them to form resolves and plans and purposes, according to his will. These resolves are then to be fulfilled. But how?

4. Fulfilled by God's Power

"That our God may make you worthy of his calling and may fulfill every resolve for good and every work of faith *by his power.*" If our resolves were fulfilled by our power, we would get the glory. But, as will be plain in just a moment, God intends to get the glory for the fulfillment of our good resolves. So he fulfills them by *his* power, not ours. Our duty is to tap into his power. Again we ask, *how?*

5. Living by Faith

"That our God may make you worthy of his calling and may fulfill every resolve for good and every *work of faith* by his power." We access God's power *by faith.* And when God fulfills a resolve for good, it becomes a work *of faith.* This is because the means by which we receive the power to fulfill the resolve, turning it into a deed, is faith. The deed or the work or the act is then called a "work of faith" or a "deed of faith" or an "act of faith."

So from God's side, the resolve becomes a deed *by God's power.* And from our side, the resolve becomes a deed *by faith*—faith *in* that power. We can think of it this way:

By *faith*
we trust God
for the power to fulfill our resolve,
and by that power,
through that *faith*,
our resolve becomes a deed or work,
a work of *faith*.

A sin is defeated, or an act of righteousness is performed, because we have looked away from ourselves and looked to God and all his powerful effects in our lives.

6. Jesus Is Glorified

"So that *the name of our Lord Jesus may be glorified in you*." God fulfills our resolves, by his power, through our faith, *so that* the name of Jesus gets glory. The text assumes that the power of God is coming to us because of Jesus—because Jesus has died for us, God's power is now not against us but for us. So when that power enables us to turn our resolves into deeds of love, Jesus and the Father get the glory.

7. We Are Glorified in Him

"So that the name of our Lord Jesus may be glorified in you, *and you in him*." As Jesus glorifies himself by purchasing for us the power of God to be made worthy of our calling, we too are being glorified. And the day will come when that slow process in this world will be completed in the twinkling of an eye, and we will "be saved to sin no more." This is the calling for which we are being made worthy, suitable, fitting.

8. It Is All of Grace

This whole process of being made worthy of our calling, and fulfilling our good resolves, and doing good works by faith in God's power, comes to us by grace. So the complete verse 12 reads, "so that the name of our Lord Jesus may be glorified in you, and you in him, *according to the grace of our God and the Lord Jesus Christ.*" It is all of grace. The power of God that comes to us moment by moment, fulfilling our resolves in works of faith, is the power of grace.

Now let me put the eight pieces together in the order that they actually work. Paul ended with the foundation of everything, "the grace of God and the Lord Jesus Christ." Let's start with the foundation and build the structure of the Christian life with these eight pieces. If you are a Christian, this is your life.

1. **Grace:** Everything starts with and is built on the grace of God.
2. **Power:** That grace is expressed in God's power toward his children.
3. **Faith:** That gracious power is appropriated, received, and tapped into by faith.
4. **Resolves fulfilled:** The effect of this power, as we trust God for it, is to fulfill our resolves for good.
5. **Works of faith:** That fulfillment turns resolves into acts, deeds, which the Bible calls works of faith. Thus, the life of the Christian is lived by faith. Christianity is not a will-power religion. We do will things: we resolve, we plan, we form purposes. But as we engage our wills to act, we look to God. And we treasure him, we love him, we trust him that the power will be given to fulfill the resolve.

6. **Made worthy:** In this way, then, we are made worthy of our calling. A life of God-dependent obedience is a life fitting, or appropriate, or suitable for our calling into God's kingdom and glory.

7. **We are glorified:** This being-made-worthy is the first stage in our being fully glorified in Christ.

8. **Jesus is glorified:** All of the above ultimately leads to Christ's being fully glorified through us.

So when you stand back and look at 2 Thessalonians 1:11–12, you are presented with this amazing panorama of the Christian life and of the meaning of existence. Everything flows from the free grace of God in Christ. And everything is moving toward the fullest glory of God in us and through us. And between the foundation of grace and the goal of glory there is the power of grace daily arriving in our lives, through faith turning daily resolves and plans and purposes into deeds of faith, and thereby fitting us for glory. Live these verses!

That's your life as a Christian. Daily, hourly, tapping into the flow of God's grace for the awakening and fulfilling of your good resolves, so that as you are made increasingly worthy of his calling—fitted for his kingdom and glory—Jesus gets more and more glory in your life.

What This Means for the Everyday

Now let me draw out this amazing picture of the Christian life what I mean by the phrase "living by faith in future grace." It's all right here in these two verses, either explicitly or implicitly.

Grace in the New Testament is not only God's disposition to do good for us when we don't deserve it (undeserved favor). It is also a power from God that acts in our lives and makes good things happen in us and for us. Paul said in verse 11 that we fulfill our resolves for good "by his power." And then he adds at the end of verse 12, "according to the grace of our God and the Lord Jesus Christ." That power that actually works in our lives to make Christ-exalting obedience possible is an extension of the grace of God.

You can see this also in 1 Corinthians 15:10: "By the *grace* of God I am what I am, and his *grace* toward me was not in vain. On the contrary, I worked harder than any of them, though it was not I, but the *grace* of God that is with me." So grace is an active, present, transformative, obedience-enabling power.

Therefore this grace, which moves in power from God to you at a point in time, is both past and future. It has *already* done something for you or in you, and therefore is past. And it is *about* to do something in you and for you, and so it is future—both five seconds away and five million years away.

God's grace is ever cascading over the waterfall of the present, from the inexhaustible river of grace coming to us from the future, into the ever-increasing reservoir of grace in the past. In the next five minutes, you will receive sustaining grace flowing to you from the future, and you will accumulate another five minutes' worth of grace in the reservoir of the past.

The proper response to the grace you have experienced in the past is gratitude—a profoundly humble and transforming spirit in itself. And the proper response to grace promised to you in the future is faith. We are thankful for past grace, and we are confident in future grace. This is where I get the idea of faith in future grace. That's what

Paul is talking about in 2 Thessalonians 2:11–12. We fulfill our good resolves by the power of grace arriving, second by second, as we trust God for it on the basis of Christ's work. And so we live in those moments by faith in the constant, unfailing arrival of future grace.

It is not wrong to say that we trust in past grace (specifically, the grace God showed us at the cross and in our new birth) but what we mean is this: *because of these acts of past grace, we believe that the river of future grace will never, ever stop flowing to us for all eternity.*

Christ died for us, and he lives for us. And because his death is all-purchasing, and his life is all-providing, grace will never stop flowing to us. Therefore, to trust in past grace means to draw from it confidence in future grace. Christ "is able to save to the uttermost those who draw near to God through him, since he always lives to make intercession for them" (Hebrews 7:25).

So our faith is founded on decisive acts of *past* redeeming grace. And that faith works in the *present*, moment by moment, to turn our resolves for good into deeds of purity and love. And the *way* that faith works is by looking *up* to God and *forward* to the boundless fountain of grace that comes to us through a river of promises for every moment of the day.

We live by faith in the ever-arriving power of future grace.

Faith in Jesus Means Being Satisfied in Him

Here's another aspect of this teaching. When we speak of faith in future grace, we mean being satisfied with all that

God promises to be for us in Christ. Jesus said, "Whoever believes in me shall never thirst" (John 6:35). In other words, *believing in me means receiving me as the satisfier of the thirst of your soul*; being satisfied with all that God promises to be for us in Christ.

Faith is not only a serious assent to the truth of God's promises, it is also a satisfying embrace of Christ in those promises. When Paul says, "I count everything as loss because of the surpassing worth of knowing Christ" (Philippians 3:8), he means that moment by moment, in every situation, Christ satisfies. "I have learned in whatever situation I am," Paul said, "to be content. I know how to be brought low, and I know how to abound. In any and every circumstance, I have learned the secret of facing plenty and hunger, abundance and need. I can do all things through him who strengthens me" (Philippians 4:11–13).

Paul is "content"—satisfied—in every circumstance. How? Because he has learned a secret: to trust God for moment-by-moment strengthening. "I can do all things through him who strengthens me." The future grace of all that God is for him in Christ, arriving every moment of his life, in every circumstance, for every need, is enough. It satisfies. He is content. That is the essence of "faith in future grace."

So when Paul says in 2 Thessalonians 1:11 that God fulfills our good resolves by his power through our faith according to his grace, he means that we defeat sin and we do righteousness by faith in future grace, that is, by being satisfied with all that God promises to be for us in Christ in the next five minutes, five weeks, five months, five years, five decades, five centuries, and five million ages of ages.

Six Examples of How God Fulfills Our Good Resolves

If you set your heart to give sacrificially and generously, the power of God to fulfill this resolve will come to you as you trust his future grace seen in promises like these. First, "My God will supply every need of yours according to his riches in glory in Christ Jesus" (Philippians 4:19). Second, "Whoever sows bountifully will also reap bountifully" (2 Corinthians 9:6). And third, "God is able to make all grace abound to you, so that having all sufficiency in all things at all times, you may abound in every good work" (2 Corinthians 9:8).

If you set your heart to return good for evil, the power of God to fulfill this resolve will come to you as you trust his future grace seen in the promise, "Blessed are you when others revile you and persecute you and utter all kinds of evil against you falsely on my account. Rejoice and be glad, for your reward is great in heaven" (Matthew 5:11–12).

If you set your heart to renounce pornography, the power of God to fulfill this resolve will come to you as you trust his future grace in these promises. "Blessed are the pure in heart, for they shall see God" (Matthew 5:8), and "It is better that you lose one of your members than that your whole body be thrown into hell" (Matthew 5:29). Much better. Wonderfully better. All-satisfyingly better.

If you set your heart to speak out for Christ when the opportunity comes, the power of God to fulfill this resolve will come to you as you trust his future grace in the promise, "Do not be anxious how you are to speak or what you are to say, for what you are to say will be given to you in that hour" (Matthew 10:19).

If you set your heart to risk your life by ministering to the needy in a dangerous place, the power of God to fulfill this resolve will come to you as you trust his future grace in the promises, "To live is Christ, and to die is gain" (Philippians 1:21), and "Do not fear those who kill the body but cannot kill the soul.... Are not two sparrows sold for a penny? And not one of them will fall to the ground apart from your Father. But even the hairs of your head are all numbered" (Matthew 10:28–30).

If you set your heart to invite some for dinner who cannot repay you, the power of God to fulfill this resolve will come to you as you trust his future grace in the promise, "You will be blessed, because they cannot repay you. For you will be repaid at the resurrection of the just" (Luke 14:13–14).

May God increase our daily faith in his inexhaustible, blood-bought, Christ-exalting future grace!

More about Living the Christian Life

BUILD YOUR LIFE ON THE MERCIES OF GOD

I appeal to you therefore, brothers, by the mercies of God, to present your bodies as a living sacrifice, holy and acceptable to God, which is your spiritual worship. —Romans 12:1

This is one of those "therefore" moments, one of Paul's "in light of everything I've just written you" statements that serve as summary and emphasis and transition. And of all the things Paul could have picked out from the first eleven chapters of Romans to emphasize and highlight as the root and foundation of your new life in Christ, he picks out *the mercies of God.*

What an amazing statement! Having written of God's wrath and righteousness and judgment, and of our fall and sin and death, and of Christ's death and resurrection, and of justification by faith alone, and of the coming of the Spirit to sanctify us and keep us, and of God's absolute sovereignty in his faithfulness to the elect and to Israel—having said all of that, Paul picks out this one great reality as the sum, or the height, of it all, and says, therefore, by *the mercies of God* I appeal to you.

This is not careless. Look at Romans 15:8–9, "For I tell you that Christ became a servant to the circumcised to show God's truthfulness, *in order to confirm the promises given to the patriarchs, and in order that the Gentiles might glorify God for his mercy.*"There it is. The aim of the entire book of Romans is that we might make the mercy of God look great among the nations. O Christian, let's build our lives on the mercies of God. Let's say, "Because of the mercies of God in Christ I will live the life of Romans chapters 12 to16." You know this is the right track here when you just walk down through chapter 12 and look at all the mercy that is going to flow out of us when we build our lives on the mercy of God.

> The one who does acts of mercy, [let him do it] with cheerfulness. (v. 8)
>
> Let love be genuine. (v. 9)
>
> Contribute to the needs of the saints. (v. 13)
>
> Bless those who persecute you. (v. 14)

Weep with those who weep. (v. 15)

Associate with the lowly. (v. 16)

Repay no one evil for evil. (v. 17)

Never avenge yourselves. (v. 19)

If your enemy is hungry, feed him; if he is thirsty, give him something to drink. (v. 20)

As we move into Romans 12–16, we are entering a world of mercy. Why? Because as believers our lives are built on something. Rooted in something. They are built on the mercies of God. Our lives are rooted in the mercies of God. Our lives are founded on the mercies of God.

The word *mercy* here implies not only forgiveness for the guilty, but especially tenderhearted compassion for the helpless and desperate. This is what we should expect after Romans chapters 1–11. Look for it in Romans 5:6–8, "For while we were still weak, at the right time Christ died for the ungodly. For one will scarcely die for a righteous person—though perhaps for a good person one would dare even to die—but God shows his love for us in that while we were still sinners, Christ died for us."

Did you hear both sides of mercy? We were weak and helpless (that's one side), and we were sinners and guilty (that's the other side). Mercy responds to both. Mercy *forgives* the guilty and mercy *pities* the helpless.

Have you built your life on that? Or maybe I should ask, have you saturated your life with that? Have the mercies of God in saving you sunk to the center and core of your life, so that you are living from a deep spring of humble, brokenhearted happiness in the God of mercy?

Would you pray for me to be this way? This is what I long for. At the core of my being—where my unpremeditated words and facial expressions and grunts and twitches come from—at the core of my being I long to be swimming, childlike, in the forgiving, compassionate mercy of God. I will pray this for you, too.

How else will we love our enemies at home and on the mission field? How else will we return good for evil when we are slandered because of our stand on the inerrancy and authority of the Bible, or on the meaning of marriage, or on racial justice, or the horror of abortion, or the message that there is no way of salvation except through Jesus Christ? If our lives are not built on and saturated by the mercies of God in Christ, how will we stay merciful and magnify the Lord?

And you know, don't you, that mercy is not spineless. Look at the first two phrases of Romans 12:9, "Let love be genuine. Abhor what is evil."

Abhor is a really strong word. When you truly love deeply, you will also hate passionately whatever destroys the beloved. But mercy that is from God weeps even as it hates. So mercy hates evil, but in our personal relationships it repays no one evil for evil (v. 17). Mercy knows what it's like to be hurt and offended, but it does not avenge itself (v. 19). Mercy knows what it's like to have enemies, but it says, "If your enemy is hungry, feed him" (v. 20).

Mercy is not weak. It has an unbreakable backbone, yet is very soft to the touch.

May God encourage you and enable you by his Spirit to build your life on the mercies of God revealed in Jesus Christ. Receive these mercies. Entrust your life to them. Embrace them for the forgiveness of your sins and all the help you need to live a life of mercy.

His Commandments Are Not Burdensome

*Everyone who believes that Jesus is the Christ has
been born of God, and everyone who loves the
Father loves whoever has been born of him.* [2] *By this
we know that we love the children of God, when
we love God and obey his commandments.* [3] *For this
is the love of God, that we keep his commandments.
And his commandments are not burdensome.* [4] *For
everyone who has been born of God overcomes the
world. And this is the victory that has overcome the
world—our faith.* [5] *Who is it that overcomes the
world except the one who believes that Jesus is the
Son of God?* (1 John 5:1–5)

This passage tells us that the commandments of God are
not burdensome. Why not? Because, "everyone who has
been born of God overcomes the world. And this is the
victory that has overcome the world—our faith. Who is
it that overcomes the world except the one who believes
that Jesus is the Son of God?" Here is our roadmap for the
journey, telling us how to get to the point in our lives where
the commandments of God are not a burden, but a joy.

Verse 4 says that two things overcome the world: 1)
everyone who has been born of God, and 2) our faith. And
verse 1 sets out the relationship between faith and new
birth: "Everyone who believes that Jesus is the Christ has
been born of God." So our new birth gives rise to faith in
the promises of Christ, this faith overcomes the world, and
that overcoming takes away the burdensomeness of the
commandments of God.

How does this work? What is the connection
between the burdensomeness of the commandments of

God and the world? It seems to be two-fold. The commandments of God are burdensome to us on the one hand because the world tempts us to believe that obeying God's commandments is not as satisfying as disobeying them (and we naturally tend to agree with the world). On the other hand, there is something in us that loves to agree with the world. Before the new birth we are "from the world" (1 John 4:5). Anything contrary to the desires of the flesh and the desires of the eyes and the pride of life is a great burden and folly to unregenerate man.

> It's a burden to be sexually chaste if you believe the message of the world that fornication or adultery really will give you more satisfaction.

> It's a burden to be honest on your tax returns if you believe the message of the world that more money will bring you satisfaction.

> It's a burden to witness to a colleague if you believe the message of the world that Christians are foolish and that getting egg on your face is to be avoided at all costs.

> It's a burden to say, "I'm sorry; I was wrong," if you believe the message of the world that more satisfaction comes from keeping up the front of strength.

But if the world could be overcome, then the commandments of God would not be burdensome. They would be the way of joy and peace and satisfaction. What can overcome the temptations of the world? What can unmask the lies of the world?

God can. And he does it by causing us to be born again so that we can see the infinite superiority of the promises of Christ over the promises of the world. The result is that we trust Christ and by trusting him overcome the temptations of the world.

Faith says to every temptation of the world, "*No. Begone!* I know where true satisfaction is to be found. God has loved me with an infinite love. He promises to work everything together for good for those who love him. He withholds no good thing from those who walk uprightly. Nothing you offer can compare to the joy of his fellowship now and the glory to be revealed hereafter. World, you have lost your power. I have become the glad slave of a Good Master. His yoke is easy and the burden of his commandments is light."

The Lord holds out many good things to you here. If you want to know that your love for others is real and not just self-deception, if you want to have the power to obey the commandments of God, if you want to find a life that is loving and at the same time not burdensome, if you want to overcome the deceptive power of the world, then consider the infinite superiority of the Son of God and put your faith in his forgiveness for your sins and his promises for your future. Whoever has the Son has life!

HEBREWS 3:12-15

Take care, brothers, lest there be in any of you an evil, unbelieving heart, leading you to fall away from the living God. [13] But exhort one another every day, as long as it is called "today," that none of you may be hardened by the deceitfulness of sin. [14] For we have come to share in Christ, if indeed we hold our original confidence firm to the end. [15] As it is said, "Today, if you hear his voice, do not harden your hearts as in the rebellion."

8

The Perseverance of the Saints

Upheaval and turmoil locally, nationally, and globally should serve as a warning to us that the day will come, sooner or later, when the hostility of man will not be containable by human force. It will burst the dam of restraint and flood to your very door. And the most urgent question for all followers of Jesus Christ will be one of endurance. Will our faith in Jesus endure? Or will we give way to fear and unbelief and anger and vengeance?

The prophet Daniel describes a time when one of the rulers of the last days, "shall speak words against the Most High, and shall *wear out* the saints of the Most High" (Daniel 7:25). And in the Book of Revelation, the apostle John describes the time by writing, "If anyone is to be taken captive, to captivity he goes; if anyone is to be slain with the sword, with the sword must he be slain. Here is a call for the *endurance* and faith of the saints" (Revelation 13:10).

The crucial question for you in those days, and in these days, is whether you will endure. Will your faith bear up under the assaults that are coming? Or will you be "worn out" and give up the faith and join the unbelieving illusion of safety? This is the question of perseverance, the question of eternal security.

This doctrine, which goes by different names, has an urgent and practical application to our life together as Christians. Some call it the doctrine of eternal security. Some call it the doctrine of perseverance. Whichever you call it, it is a process and it is a community project. For you and I are essential to one another, helping each other persevere to the end in faith, so that we do not take the alternative path—making shipwreck of our souls.

Three Points on Perseverance

The signature text on this doctrine is Hebrews 3:12–15. I would like to sketch a three-point theology of perseverance based on these four verses and their implications for your life. Then I will show the wider basis for this in Scripture, and its relation to the cross of our Lord Jesus.

The Call to Endure is Real

"Take care, brothers, lest there be in any of you an evil, unbelieving heart, leading you to fall away from the living God" (Hebrews 3:12). This is a clear call to all believers ("brothers") to persevere in faith. Not to give way to unbelief. Not to "wear out." It's a call to endure, to last, to keep the faith to the end. It urges us: Don't let your heart become evil and unbelieving; don't fall away from the living God. This is a real danger spoken to the church. Blow it off because your doctrine of eternal security won't allow it, and you place yourself in the greatest of dangers.

We Each Are a Means for One Another's Endurance

"But [in contrast to giving way to a heart of unbelief] exhort one another every day, as long as it is called 'today,' that none of you may be hardened by the deceitfulness of sin" (Hebrews 3:13). Then the writer actually does for us what he just told us to do for one another. He gives us an exhortation from Psalm 95:7–8, "Today, if you hear his voice, do not harden your hearts as in the rebellion" (v. 15).

So one of the essential means of not becoming hardened by the deceitfulness of sin—of not having an evil, unbelieving heart—is for Christians to imitate this model of personal exhortation, as other believers around you speaking faith-sustaining words into your life. Your family, your friends, your church, your small group. "Exhort one another every day." Speak words of faith-sustaining truth into each other's lives. Paul said to only let out of your mouth what is "good for building up, as fits the occasion, that it may give grace to those who hear" (Ephesians 4:29).

In other words, the second point in this theology of perseverance is that God has designed his church so that its members endure to the end, in faith, largely *by means of* giving and receiving faith-sustaining words to and from each other. You and I are the instruments by which God preserves the faith of his children. Perseverance is a community project. Just like God is not going to evangelize the world without human, faith-awakening voices, neither is he going to preserve his church without human, faith-sustaining voices. And clearly from the words, "exhort one another" (v. 13) it means all of us, not just preachers. We depend on each other to endure in faith to the end.

Persevering in Faith is Evidence that We Are in Christ

Exhort each other, and help each other hold onto confidence, "for [because] we *have come* to share in Christ, if indeed we *hold* our original confidence firm to the end" (v. 14). This is one of the most important verses in the book of Hebrews, because it establishes that if a person *has come* to share in Christ, that person will most certainly persevere to the end in faith.

Look at the logic and the verb tenses carefully. Everything hangs on this. "We *have come* to share in Christ, if indeed we *hold* our original confidence firm to the end" (v. 14). Notice that he does not say, "if we hold our confidence to the end." He says, "our *original* confidence." Which means that enduring to the end doesn't *earn you* a share in Christ. It proves you *already had* a share in Christ, a share granted you by grace through faith. Perseverance is the evidence of being born again in Christ, not the means to it.

Or to put the same point negatively, if you don't hold your confidence in Christ to the end, what would it show? It would show that you *had not* "come to share in Christ." So the negative of verse 14 would read, "We *have not come* to share in Christ, if indeed we *do not hold* our original confidence firm to the end."

Do you see what this implies about eternal security? It says that if you have come to share in Christ—if you are born again, if you are truly converted, if you are justified and forgiven through saving faith—you cannot fail to persevere. You *will* hold your confidence in Christ to the end.

The logic is identical with 1 John 2:19. "They went out from us, but they were not of us; for if they had been of us, they would have continued with us. But they went out, that it might become plain that they all are not of us." The statement, "if they had been of us, they would have continued with us," is essentially the same as "if you truly share in Christ, you will hold your confidence to the end."

So here's the summary of this three-point theology of perseverance.

1. Don't let your heart become evil and unbelieving, because if you do, you will fall away from the living God and perish forever.
2. As a means of protecting each other from such an evil heart of unbelief, speak sin-defeating, faith-sustaining words into each other's lives every day.
3. This warning and exhortation is not there because a person who truly belongs to Christ can be lost, but because perseverance is the evidence that you truly belong to Christ. If you fall away, you show that you never truly shared in Christ. And God will never let this happen to those who have shared in Christ.

"Those whom he predestined he also called, and those whom he called he also justified, and those whom he justified he also glorified" (Romans 8:30). Between eternity past in God's predestination, and eternity future in God's glorification, none is lost. No one who is predestined for sonship fails to be called. And no one who is called fails to be justified. And no one who is justified fails to be glorified. This is an unbreakable steel chain of divine covenant faithfulness.

Therefore Paul says, "And I am sure of this, that he who began a good work in you will bring it to completion at the day of Jesus Christ" (Philippians 1:6). And he states further that God "will sustain you to the end, guiltless in the day of our Lord Jesus Christ. God is faithful, by whom you were called into the fellowship of his Son, Jesus Christ our Lord" (1 Corinthians 1:8–9). These are the promises of our God who cannot lie. Those who are born again are as secure as God is faithful.

Perseverance and the Cross

What is the connection between this security—this promised perseverance—and the cross of our Lord Jesus? Just before Jesus shed his blood for sinners, he lifted up the cup at the Last Supper and said, "This cup that is poured out for you is the new covenant in my blood" (Luke 22:20). What that means is that the new covenant, promised most explicitly in Jeremiah 31 and 32, was secured and sealed by the blood of Jesus. The new covenant comes true because Jesus died to establish it.

And what does the new covenant secure for all who belong to Christ? *Perseverance in faith to the end.* Consider Jeremiah 32:40, "I will make with them an everlasting covenant, that I will not turn away from doing good to them. *And I will put the fear of me in their hearts, that they may not turn from me.*" The everlasting covenant—the new covenant—includes the unbreakable promise, "I will put the fear of me in their hearts, that they may not turn from me." That they may not: will not, shall not. Christ sealed this covenant with his blood. He purchased your perseverance.

If you are persevering in faith today, you owe it to

the blood of Jesus. The Holy Spirit, who is working in you to preserve your faith, honors the purchase of Jesus. God the Spirit works in us what God the Son obtained for us. The Father planned it. Jesus bought it. The Spirit applies it. And all three persons of the Trinity act infallibly. God is totally committed to the eternal security of his blood-bought children.

Applying Community

As an elaboration of point two above, let us now underscore our application for this chapter. We see in Hebrews 3:13 that God has united the certainty of security with the necessity of community: "Exhort *one another* every day, as long as it is called 'today,' that none of you may be hardened by the deceitfulness of sin." To put a finer point on an earlier statement: *blood-bought* eternal security is a *blood-bought* community project.

That may sound as though our security is fragile, since our communal life is always imperfect. But it is not fragile. It is no more fragile than the sovereign ability of God to bring others into your life and to send you into theirs. God will sovereignly preserve all who belong to Christ. And he will do it in no small part through the faith-sustaining ministry of other believers.

For married Christian couples, this means that God, not man ("what God has joined together"), has already put you in households designed for daily faith-sustaining, sin-defeating ministry of the word to each other—husbands and wives, parents and children.

Let me give you some examples of what it means for husbands and wives to "do" Hebrews 3:13 for each other.

For Husbands

Love your wife sacrificially and cherish her as a reflection of the love of Christ for the church (Ephesians 5:25, 29). It will sustain her faith to experience this.

Be alert to and discern your wife's spiritual, emotional, relational, and physical needs, and make the effort to meet those needs—directly or indirectly (Hebrews 3:12–13; 1 Peter 3:7).

Seek to build up your wife with biblical knowledge, through your own words, and by your encouragement and help in connecting her with biblical teaching (John 8:32; Ephesians 4:25–30).

Encourage and help your wife engage in ministry at church and in the world (Proverbs 31:20; Ephesians 4:11–12; 1 Timothy 5:9–10).

For Wives

Be alert to your husband's spiritual condition and pray earnestly for him (1 Samuel 25:1–35; Hebrews 3:12–13).

Encourage your husband by affirming evidences of grace in his life (Romans 15:2; Ephesians 4:29; Hebrews 10:24–25). It will sustain his faith to hear this.

Support him in all his leadership efforts, and be responsive to every effort he makes to lead spiritually (Ephesians 5:21–24; 1 Peter 3:1–6).

Share from your life and your meditation the things God is teaching you about Christ and his ways (Romans 15:13–14; 1 Thessalonians 4:18).

Join him in serious conversation with respect and wisdom (Proverbs 31:26; Romans 15:2; 1 Thessalonians 5:11).

No one knows him like you know him, so suggest to him people and resources that may be of help to him (Genesis 2:18; Proverbs 31:12; Acts 20:32).

Humbly and hopefully help him be aware of unhelpful habits or sins you may see in his life (Hebrews 3:12–13; James 5:16).

I know this assumes that you are both believers, and that you are both willing. And I know that's not true of every married couple. But it is what God calls us to pray toward and move toward for the sake of our spouses and our children's perseverance in faith. Eternal security is a family project.

For Everyone

And here's a word to all of us, the single and the married. God did not design marriage to replace the church, and he didn't design families to replace friendships. Every married man needs other believing men in his life. Every married woman needs other believing women in her life. Young people need other believing young people. And single people need married people as well single people in their lives. Families are not substitutes for any of these relationships.

The blood-bought church of Christ is the new, supernatural family. This is another astonishing truth that turns the world upside down. Single people, married people, old and young, rich and poor, every ethnicity—all can find brothers and sisters in the church. Marriage is temporary. Parenting is temporary. But the church—the new family—is eternal.

More about Perseverance of the Saints

SETTLING OUR SECURITY IN GOD ALONE

One obstacle to enjoying the security we have in Christ is the hard texts in the New Testament that seem to contradict it. Just when we start to feel that we are eternally secure in his love, along comes a passage of Scripture that threatens us and seems to rob us of security. I don't think there will be any deep, abiding sense of security in God until we own up to these passages of Scripture and see how they relate to the assurance of God's love and power. Consider this sampling from nine New Testament books.

> **Romans:** Unbelieving Israelites "were broken off because of their unbelief, but you stand fast only through faith. So do not become proud, but fear. For if God did not spare the natural branches, neither will he spare you" (Romans 11:20–21).

> **First Corinthians:** "Let anyone who thinks that he stands take heed lest he fall" (1 Corinthians 10:12). Also, "the gospel I preached to you... by which you are being saved, if you hold fast to the word I preached to you—unless you believed in vain" (1 Corinthians 15:1–2).

Second Corinthians: "Examine yourselves, to see whether you are in the faith. Test yourselves. Or do you not realize this about yourselves, that Jesus Christ is in you?—unless indeed you fail to meet the test!" (2 Corinthians 13:5).

Galatians: "Let us not grow weary of doing good, for in due season we will reap, if we do not give up" (Galatians 6:9).

Philippians: "Work out your own salvation with fear and trembling" (Philippians 2:12).

Colossians: "You who once were alienated and hostile in mind… [Christ] has now reconciled… in order to present you holy and blameless… if indeed you continue in the faith, stable and steadfast, not shifting from the hope of the gospel" (Colossians 1:21–23).

Hebrews: "Strive for peace with everyone, and for the holiness without which no one will see the Lord" (Hebrews 12:14).

First Peter: "If you call on him as Father who judges impartially according to each one's deeds, conduct yourselves with fear throughout the time of your exile" (1 Peter 1:17).

Revelation: "Be faithful unto death, and I will give you the crown of life" (Revelation 2:10).

All these passages teach that the *test of genuineness* for the Christian *is* perseverance in faith and holiness of life. They warn us sternly against assuming eternal security in the absence of lasting faith and lives of love. To offer someone a sense of security without these indispensable realities is to offer false security at the price of certain destruction.

It would be a terrible misunderstanding to imagine that these verses are intended to threaten our security in God. Exactly the opposite is the case. *They are written to threaten our security in everything but God.* If you find your security in health, the Bible is a threat to you. If you find your security in your family or job or money or education, the Bible is a threat to you. And in threatening all these utterly inadequate foundations of security, the Bible drives us relentlessly and lovingly back to the one and only eternal and unshakable foundation for security: God. All the threats and warnings of the Bible declare with one voice that sin is an effort to feel secure in anything other than God.

Therefore when God demands, on the one hand, that *we must turn from sinning or we will die,* and on the other hand demands that *if we feel eternally secure in his love we will live,* he is not demanding two different things. Why? Because sin is what you do when you replace security in God with other things. So when God threatens our sense of security in the things of the world, it's because he wants us to feel secure—exclusively and entirely—in his love and power. The threats and promises of Scripture have one message: *seek your security in God alone.*

Security in God Alone

Ephesians 1:11–14 is one of the clearest statements in the Bible about God's desire that his people find their security in him alone, that we feel secure in his love and power.

In him we have obtained an inheritance, having

been predestined according to the purpose
of him who works all things according to the
counsel of his will, [12] so that we who were the
first to hope in Christ might be to the praise of
his glory. [13] In him you also, when you heard the
word of truth, the gospel of your salvation, and
believed in him, were sealed with the promised
Holy Spirit, [14] who is the guarantee of our inheritance until we acquire possession of it, to the
praise of his glory.

The first and most important thing to see in these
three verses is that they begin and end with God's ultimate purpose, to glorify himself. We were destined and
appointed to live "to the praise of his glory" (v. 12). He has
guaranteed our inheritance, again, "to the praise of his
glory" (v. 14). The most basic fact about the righteousness
of God is that he has an unwavering commitment to his
own glory. Everything he does, he does to heighten the
intensity with which his people praise him for his glory.

The second thing to see in this passage is that the
people whose inheritance God guarantees are the people
who *believe* the gospel: you who have "believed in him,
were sealed" (v. 13). There is a direct connection between
believing God's word and living for the praise of his glory.
One of the greatest ways to honor people is to trust them,
and since God is committed to his own honor above all
things, he is therefore utterly committed to those who
trust him.

The third thing, then, to see from this text, is just
what you would expect. Because God does all things for
the praise of his glory, and because believing his word

magnifies that glory, God takes decisive steps to secure for himself the magnification of his glory forever. And he does this by *sealing* believers with the Holy Spirit, and *guaranteeing* that we will come to our full inheritance praising his glory.

God is so passionately committed to having a people for his own possession, a people who live forever for the praise of his glory, that he is not about to let our eternal destiny depend on our native powers of willing or doing. He commissions his Holy Spirit to enter our lives and to make us secure forever.

Sealed and Guaranteed, Forever

There are two great words in our Ephesians passage that aim to help us feel secure in God's love and power—*sealed* and *guarantee*. Let's see if we can unseal this word *sealed* and look inside. What does it mean that believers have been "sealed with the promised Holy Spirit" (v. 13)? The word is used at least three different ways in the New Testament.

1. In Matthew 27:66, the tomb of Jesus was secured by *sealing* it and putting guards around it. In Revelation 20:3, God throws Satan into a pit and *seals* it over so he can't escape. So one meaning of *seal* is locking something up, closing it in.
2. Another kind of use is found in Romans 4:11, where Abraham's circumcision is called the sign and *seal* of the righteousness he had by faith. And in 1 Corinthians 9:2, Paul says that his converts are the *seal* of his apostleship. So a second meaning of *seal* is a sign of authenticity.

3. A third use is found in Revelation 7:3, where the
   seal of God is put on the forehead of God's servants
   to protect them from the wrath coming upon the
   world. Here, the word indicates a protective mark of
   ownership.

So what did Paul mean in Ephesians 1:13 when he said that
believers are sealed with the Holy Spirit? No matter which
of these meanings you use, the basic truth is the same.

1. If the Spirit *seals shut*, he seals in faith and seals out
   unbelief and apostasy.
2. If the Spirit seals us as a *sign of authenticity*, then he
   himself is that sign, the Spirit's work in our life being
   God's trademark. In other words, our eternal sonship
   is real and authentic if we have the Spirit. The third
   person of the Trinity is the sign of divine reality in
   our lives.
3. If the Spirit *marks us with God's seal*, he protects us
   from evil forces, which won't dare to enter a person
   bearing the mark of God's own possession.

However you come at the message contained in this word
sealed, it is a message of safety and security in God's love
and power. God sends the Holy Spirit as a *preserving* seal
to lock in our faith, as an *authenticating* seal to validate
our sonship, and as a *protecting* seal to keep out destructive
forces. The point is that God wants us to feel secure and
safe in his love and power.

The other word Paul uses to drive this home is the
word *guarantee* in verse 14. "You were sealed with the
promised Holy Spirit which is the *guarantee* of our inheritance." Noël and I ran out of gas once in downtown

Minneapolis. I ran to a nearby service station and bor-
rowed a can with two dollars's worth of gas. I said I would
be right back and buy fifteen dollars's worth. But I had to
leave my driver's license. Why? Because it was a *guarantee*
I would come back and finish my business. They knew that
my driver's license was valuable enough to me to give them
a sense of security that I would come back with their can.
So then, what is God saying to us when he gives us his
Holy Spirit and calls him a guarantee or a down-payment?
He is saying, in effect,

> My great desire for those who believe in me is
> that you feel secure in my love. I have chosen
> you before the foundation of the world. I have
> predestined you to be my children forever. I have
> redeemed you by the blood of my Son. And I
> have put my Spirit in you as a seal and a guar-
> antee. Therefore, you will receive the inheritance
> and you will praise the glory of my grace forever
> and ever. And I tell you this here in Ephesians 1
> because I want you to feel secure in my love and
> my power. I don't promise you an easy life. In
> fact, through many tribulations you must enter
> the kingdom. I don't promise always to speak in
> soft tones of approval, but to warn you in love
> whenever you begin to seek security in anything
> but me.
>
> So let me say it again: I have chosen you; I have
> predestined you; I have redeemed you; I have
> sealed you by my Spirit. Your inheritance is sure,
> because I am passionately committed to magni-
> fying the glory of my grace in your salvation.

It is as if God sings to us and for us,

> When peace like a river attendeth your way,
> When sorrows like sea billows roll,
> Whatever your lot—I have taught you to say,
> It is well, it is well, with your soul.

GENESIS 1:26–31

Then God said, "Let us make man in our image, after our likeness. And let them have dominion over the fish of the sea and over the birds of the heavens and over the livestock and over all the earth and over every creeping thing that creeps on the earth." [27] So God created man in his own image, in the image of God he created him; male and female he created them. [28] And God blessed them. And God said to them, "Be fruitful and multiply and fill the earth and subdue it, and have dominion over the fish of the sea and over the birds of the heavens and over every living thing that moves on the earth." [29] And God said, "Behold, I have given you every plant yielding seed that is on the face of all the earth, and every tree with seed in its fruit. You shall have them for food. [30] And to every beast of the earth and to every bird of the heavens and to everything that creeps on the earth, everything that has the breath of life, I have given every green plant for food." And it was so. [31] And God saw everything that he had made, and behold, it was very good. And there was evening and there was morning, the sixth day.

9
Biblical Manhood and Womanhood

One of the long-standing trademarks of Bethlehem has been the way the church understands God's purposes for how men and women relate to each other in family and church and society. The most common name for this understanding is *complementarian*, based on *complement*. It takes the view that, when it comes to human sexuality, the greatest display of God's glory, and the greatest joy of human relationships, and the greatest fruitfulness in ministry come about when the deep differences between men and women are embraced and celebrated as complementary to each other. Because these differences complete and beautify each other.

So complementarians use this label to position our perspective and way of life between two kinds of error. One is the various abuses of women under male domination, and the other is the negation of gender differences that we see as having beautiful significance.

This means that, on the one hand, complementarians acknowledge, lament, and deplore, in all its forms, the personal and systematic mistreatment, disrespect, abuse, and exploitation of women and girls. On the other hand, complementarians lament feminist and egalitarian impulses that minimize God-given differences between men and women, as these impulses tend to dismantle the order God has designed for the flourishing of human life.

Complementarians resist the impulses of a chauvinistic, dominating, and abusive culture; as well as the impulses of a largely gender-blind, gender-leveling, unisex culture. And we take our stand between these two ways of life, not because the middle ground is a safe place (it is emphatically not), but because we think this is the good plan of God in the Bible for men and women. "Very good," as he says in Genesis 1.

In fact, I would say that feminism's attempt to remedy the male abuse of women by nullifying gender differences has backfired, producing millions of men whom women either cannot enjoy because of their unmanliness, or cannot endure because of their distorted, brutal manliness. From the complementarian view, if we fail to teach boys and girls about the truth and beauty and value of their differences, and how to live these out, those differences mature in ways that are unhealthy and dysfunctional. The result is another generation of young adults who simply do not know what it means to be a mature man or woman. The cultural price we pay for this is enormous.

I will move now from the general to the specific, offering a word about being human, an illustration about being male and female, and then a specific text to show the biblical roots of complementarianism.

Grandeur of Being Human

On the evening of July 13, 1980, my first Sunday at Bethlehem Baptist Church, I gave a message titled, "Life Is Not Trivial." In it I said,

> Every human being now and then feels a longing
> that life not dribble away like a leaky faucet.
> You've all tasted the desire that day-to-day life
> be more than a series of trifles. It can happen
> when you are reading a poem, when you are
> kneeling in your closet, when you are standing
> by the lakeside at sunset. It very often happens
> at birth and death." I also quoted Moses from
> Deuteronomy 32:46, "Lay to heart all the words
> which I enjoin upon you this day, that you may
> command them to your children, that they may
> be careful to do all the words of this law. For *it is
> no trifle* for you but it is your life.

Deep in every God-created human being, with each of us bearing the insignia of humanity in the image of God, there is a longing for life not to be meaningless—not to be trivial, frivolous, inconsequential. Consider this thought from crime novelist Agatha Christie (1896–1976), "I like living. I have sometimes been wildly, despairingly, acutely miserable, racked with sorrow, but through it all, I still know quite certainly, that just to be alive, is a grand thing."

I think this is wonderfully true. To be a living human being is a grand thing. Maybe you have had one of those rare and wonderful moments such as I have occasionally enjoyed. I'll be standing by a window, or a door, or anywhere, and suddenly, unbidden and powerful, comes the

awakening: *I am alive. I am alive. Not like a tree or rabbit,
but like a human being. I am thinking, feeling, longing, regret-
ting, grieving. Alive. Made in the very image of God. And this
is a grand thing.*

It is indeed a grand thing. And part of the grandeur
of being a living human being created in the image of God
is that you are either male or female. "God created man in
his own image, in the image of God he created him; male
and female he created them" (Genesis 1:27). Nobody is a
generic, undifferentiated human being. There is no such
thing, and God never intended that there be. God creates
male human beings and female human beings. And this is
a grand thing.

It is a travesty, however, to depict these two human
natures as if God's only design in establishing gender
differences was for making and nursing babies. The
differences are far too many and far too deep for such
a superficial explanation. A woman is a woman to the
depths of her humanity. And a man is a man to the depths
of his humanity. And this is a grand thing. So my first
point is that God has done a grand thing in making us
male and female in his image. Don't diminish this. Delight
in it. Glory in being alive as the male or female person you
are.

Parable of Differences

Let me create an illustration to portray some of the differences between manhood and womanhood. A picture may
be worth a thousand words; even a word picture.

Suppose that a young man and woman at an urban
church, each of them say 20 years old, find themselves

chatting before the worship service. He likes what he hears and sees, and says, "Are you sitting with anyone?" They sit together. They notice how each other engage with God in worship.

When the service is over, as they are preparing to leave, he says, "Do you have any lunch plans? I'd love to treat you to lunch." At that point she can signal she is not interested, "I do have some plans. But thanks." Or she can signal the opposite, "I do, but let me make a call. I think I can change them. I'd love to go." And that second option is what she chooses.

Neither has a car, so he suggests they walk to a café about 10 minutes from the church. As they walk, he finds out that she has a black belt in martial arts; that she is one of the best in the state. As they are approaching the café, two men block their way ominously and say, "Pretty girl-friend you've got there. We'd like her purse and your wallet. In fact, she's so pretty we'd like her."

The thought goes through his head, *she can whip these guys.* But instead of stepping behind her, he takes her arm, pulls her back behind him, and says, "If you're going to touch her, it will be over my dead body." When they make their move, he tackles them both and tells her to run.

The two men knock him unconscious, but before they know what hit them, she has put them both on their backs with some teeth knocked out. By now a small crowd has gathered, and someone has called 911. When the police and ambulance come, she gets in the ambulance with the young man, just regaining consciousness. On the way to the hospital she has one principal thought: this is the kind of man I want to marry.

The main point of that story is to illustrate that the

deeper differences of manhood and womanhood are not superior or inferior *competencies*. They are, rather, deep *dispositions* or *inclinations* written on the heart (albeit often in a very distorted way due to sin and the fall). But notice three crucial things.

First, the young man took the initiative: he asked if he could sit with her, asked if she would like to go to lunch, and suggested the place and how to get there. She saw clearly what he was doing, and responded freely according to her desires. She joined the dance. This says nothing about who has superior competencies in planning. God writes the impulse to lead on a man's heart, and the wisdom to discern it and enjoy it on a woman's heart.

Second, he said that he wanted to treat her to lunch; he's paying. This sends a signal from the young man, as if he is saying, "I think that's part of my responsibility. In this little drama of life I initiate, I provide." She understands and approves. She supports his initiative and graciously accepts the offer to be provided for. She takes the next step in the choreography. And this says nothing about who is wealthier or more capable of earning. It is what God's man feels he must do.

Third, when facing those assailants, it was irrelevant to his masculine soul that she was far better at self-defense. What emerged in the urgency of the moment was his deep, God-given, masculine impulse to protect her. It certainly wasn't his superior competency, and it wasn't foolish machismo. It was a matter of manhood. She saw it. And she felt not belittled by it, but honored, and she loved it.

At the heart of mature manhood is the God-given sense (disposition, inclination) that the primary responsibility (not sole responsibility) lies with him when it comes to leadership-initiative, provision, and protection.

And at the heart of mature womanhood is the God-given sense (disposition, inclination) that none of this implies her inferiority, but that it will be a beautiful thing to come alongside such a man and gladly affirm and receive this kind of leadership and provision and protection.

Scripture on These Differences

For those who disagree with this complementarian view, the likely criticism is that the gender differences I'm presenting as innate are all culturally determined, not innate and not from God. Complementarians, they would say, are just reflecting the home they grew up in and the biases of their childhood.

That's possible. Everyone brings assumptions and preferences to this issue. So the real question is, does God reveal his will about these things in his word?

Let's look first at a biblical text dealing with marriage, and then at one dealing with the church. In both texts Christlike, humble, loving, sacrificial men are called to take primary responsibility for leadership, provision, and protection. And women are called to come alongside these men, support that leadership, and advance the kingdom of Christ with the full range of their gifts as laid out in Scripture.

First, a text on marriage and the home.

Wives, submit to your own husbands, as to the Lord. [23] For the husband is the head of the wife even as Christ is the head of the church, his body, and is himself its Savior. [24] Now as the church submits to Christ, so also wives should submit in everything to their husbands. [25] Husbands, love your wives, as Christ loved the church and gave himself up for her, [26] that he might sanctify her, having cleansed her by the washing of water with the word, [27] so that he might present the church to himself in splendor, without spot or wrinkle or any such thing, that she might be holy and without blemish. [28] In the same way husbands should love their wives as their own bodies. He who loves his wife loves himself. [29] For no one ever hated his own flesh, but nourishes and cherishes it, just as Christ does the church, [30] because we are members of his body. [Then, quoting Genesis 2:24] [31] "Therefore a man shall leave his father and mother and hold fast to his wife, and the two shall become one flesh." [32] This mystery is profound, and I am saying that it refers to Christ and the church. [33] However, let each one of you love his wife as himself, and let the wife see that she respects her husband. (Ephesians 5:22–33)

Here are four observations drawn from this text.

1. Marriage is a dramatization of Christ's relationship to his church. "This mystery is profound, and I am saying that it refers to Christ and the church" (v. 32).
2. In this drama, the husband takes his cues from

Christ and the wife takes her cues from God's will for the church. "Husbands, love your wives, as Christ loved the church and gave himself up for her" (v. 25). "Wives, submit to your own husbands, as to the Lord. For the husband is the head of the wife even as Christ is the head of the church" (v. 22).

3. So the primary responsibility for initiative and leadership in the home is to come from the husband, who is taking his cues from Christ, the head. And it is clear that this is not about rights and power, but about responsibility and sacrifice: "as Christ loved the church and gave himself up for her" (v. 25). No abuse. No bossiness. No authoritarianism. No arrogance. Here is a man whose pride has been broken by his own need for a Savior, and he is willing to bear the burden of leadership given to him by his Master, no matter how heavy the load. Godly women see this and are glad.

4. This leadership in the home involves the sense of primary responsibility for nourishing provision and tender protection. "For no one ever hated his own flesh (that is, his wife), but nourishes and cherishes it, just as Christ does the church" (v. 29). The word *nourishes* implies nourishing provision. And the word *cherishes* implies tender protection. This is what Christ does for his bride. This is what the godly husband feels the primary responsibility to do for his wife and family.

So a complementarian concludes that biblical headship for the husband is the divine calling to take primary responsibility for Christlike servant-leadership, protection, and

provision in the home. And biblical submission for the
wife is the divine calling to honor and affirm her husband's
leadership and help carry it through according to her gifts.
"A helper fit for him," as Genesis 2:18 says.

I won't develop here the arguments for how this
applies to the church. Instead, I will just make some
summary comments about how complementarians see it.

In 1 Timothy 2:12 Paul says, "I do not permit a woman
to teach or to exercise authority over a man." In the larger
context of Scripture, we take this to mean that the primary
responsibility for governance and teaching in the church
should be carried by spiritual men. These are the two func-
tions that distinguish elders from deacons: governing (1
Timothy 5:17) and teaching (1 Timothy 3:2). So the clearest
way we apply this overall teaching is to say that the elders
of the church should be spiritual men.

In other words, since the church is the family of God,
the realities of headship and submission that we saw in
marriage (Ephesians 5:22–33) have their counterparts in
the church. In 1 Timothy 2:12, *authority* refers to the divine
calling of spiritual, gifted men to take primary responsibility as elders for Christlike servant-leadership and teaching
in the church. And in Ephesians 5, *submit* refers to the
divine calling of the rest of the church, both men and
women, to submit *to* Christ by honoring and affirming the
leadership and teaching of the elders, so as to be equipped
by them for the hundreds of ministries available to men
and women in the service *of* Christ.

That last point is very important. For men and women
who have a heart to minister—to save souls and heal
broken lives and resist evil and meet needs—the fields
of opportunity are simply endless. God intends for the

entire church to be mobilized in ministry, male and female. Nobody is to simply stay at home watching soaps and ballgames while the world burns.

The biblical picture of manhood and womanhood is a call for men and women to realize what a grand thing it is to be a man created in the image of God, and it is an equally grand thing to be a woman created in the image of God. But since the burden of primary responsibility lies on the men, here I will challenge them.

Men, do you have a moral vision for your families, a zeal for the house of the Lord, a magnificent commitment to the advancement of the kingdom, an articulate dream for the mission of the church, and a tenderhearted tenacity to make it real? You can't lead a godly woman without this. She is a grand being!

There are countless such men in the church today—but many more are needed. When the Lord visits his church and creates a mighty army of deeply spiritual, humble, strong, Christlike men committed to the word of God and the mission of the church, the vast army of women will rejoice over the leadership of these men and enter into a joyful partnership. And that will be a grand thing.

More about Biblical Manhood and Womanhood

CONFLICT AND CONFUSION AFTER THE FALL

The fact that God created us in his image, as male and female, implies six important things: equality of personhood; equality of dignity; mutual respect; harmony; complementarity; and a unified destiny. Let's briefly define each of these.

Equality of Personhood

Equality of personhood means that a man is not less a person than a woman because he has hair on his chest like a gorilla, and a woman is not less a person because she has no hair on her chest like a fish. They are equal in their personhood, and their differences don't change that basic truth.

Equality of Dignity

Equality of dignity means that they are to be equally honored as humans in the image of God. Peter says, "honor everyone" (1 Peter 2:17). There is an honor to be paid to persons simply because they are humans. There is even an honor that we owe to the most despicable of criminals, just because they are human and not canine. And that honor belongs to male and female equally.

Mutual Respect

Mutual respect means that men and women should be equally zealous to respect and honor each other. Respect should never flow in just one direction. Created in the image of God, male and female should look at each other with a kind of awe—an awe that is tainted but not destroyed by sin.

Harmony

Harmony means that there should be peaceful cooperation between men and women. We should find ways to oil the gears of our relationships so that there is teamwork and rapport and mutual helpfulness and joy.

Complementarity

Complementarity means that the music of our relationships should not be merely the sound of singing in unison. It should be the integrated, harmonized sound of soprano and bass, alto and tenor. It means that the differences of male and female will be respected and affirmed and valued. It means that male and female will not try to duplicate each other, but will highlight in each other the unique qualities that make for mutual enrichment.

Unified Destiny

Unified destiny means that male and female, when they come to faith in Christ, are "heirs with you of the grace of life" (1 Peter 3:7). We are destined for an equal enjoyment of the revelation of the glory of God in the age to come.

In creating human beings as male and female in his image, God had something wonderful in mind. He still has it in mind. And in Jesus Christ he means to redeem this vision from the ravages of sin.

Understanding the Curse

I want you to sense very keenly what the conflict is between men and women, and how great the confusion is today about what it means to be a man or a woman.

Let's look at Genesis 3:16. Adam and Eve have both sinned against God. They have distrusted his goodness and turned away from him to depend on their own wisdom for how to be happy. So they have rejected his word and eaten the fruit of the tree of the knowledge of good and evil. God calls them to account, and describes to them what the curse will be on human life because of sin. God says to the woman, "I will surely multiply your pain in childbearing;

in pain you shall bring forth children. Your desire shall
be contrary to your husband, but he shall rule over you"
(Genesis 3:16).

This is a description of the curse. It is *a description of
misery, not a model for marriage.* God is saying that this is
the way it's going to be in history where sin has the upper
hand. But what is larger point here? What is the *nature* of
this ruined relationship after sin?

The key comes from recognizing the connection
between the last words of Genesis 3:16 and the last words
of Genesis 4:7. In the latter verse, God warns Cain about
his resentment and anger against Abel, and tells him
that sin is about to get the upper hand in his life. "Sin is
crouching at the door. Its desire is contrary to you, but you
must rule over it."

The parallel here, between 3:16 and 4:7, is amazingly
close. The words are virtually the same in Hebrew, but you
can see this in the English as well. In 3:16 God says to the
woman, "Your desire shall be contrary to your husband, but
he shall rule over you." In 4:7 God says to Cain that sin's
"desire is contrary to you, but you must rule over it."

This is important to see because it shows us more
clearly what is meant by *desire* in these two verses. When
4:7 says that sin is crouching at the door of Cain's heart,
like a lion, and that its desire is contrary to him, it means
that sin wants to overpower him. It wants to defeat him
and subdue him and make him the slave of sin.

Now when we go back to 3:16, we should probably see
the same meaning in the sinful desire of woman. When
it says, "Your desire shall be contrary to your husband," it
means that when sin has the upper hand in woman, she
will desire to overpower or subdue or exploit man. And

when sin has the upper hand in man, he will respond in like manner and with his strength subdue her, or rule over her.

So what is really described in the curse of 3:16 is the ugly conflict between male and female that has marked so much of human history. Maleness as God created it has been depraved and corrupted by sin. Femaleness as God created it has been depraved and corrupted by sin. The essence of sin is self-reliance and self-exaltation, first in rebellion against God, and then in exploitation of each other.

So the essence of corrupted maleness is the self-aggrandizing effort to subdue and control and exploit women for its own private desires. And the essence of corrupted femaleness is the self-aggrandizing effort to subdue and control and exploit men for its own private desires. And the difference is found mainly in the different weaknesses that we can exploit in one another.

As a rule, men have more brute strength than women and thus they can rape and abuse and threaten and sit around and snap their fingers. It's fashionable to say these sorts of things today. But it's just as true that women are sinners. We are in God's image, male and female; and we are depraved, male and female. Women may not have as much brute strength as men, but she knows ways to subdue him. She can very often run circles around him with her words. And where her words fail, she knows the weakness of his lust and pride.

If you have any doubts about the power of sinful woman to control sinful man, just reflect for a moment on the number one marketing force in the world—the female body. Female imagery can be and has been used to sell anything and everything to men, by appealing to a universal weakness of men. It's true that the exploitation of women by sinful men is conspicuous because it is often harsh and violent. But a moment's reflection will show you that the exploitation of men by sinful women is just as pervasive in our society. The difference is that Western society sinfully sanctions the one perversity and permits the other. (Some societies do just the opposite.)

Different Movements in a Marvelous Dance

This is not the way God meant it to be—before sin, when man and woman were still fully dependent on him for how to live. Today's tension between the sexes is the result of rebellion against God. How, then, did God mean it to be? What was the relationship between Adam and Eve supposed to look like before sin entered the world? We've seen part of the answer: they were created in the image of God according to Genesis 1:27, so the relationship they had was supposed to be governed by equality of personhood, equality of dignity, mutual respect, harmony, complementarity, and a unified destiny.

But that's only part of the answer.

It's like saying to a man and woman who are ballet dancers, "Remember, you are both equally accomplished dancers; you are equally regarded among your peers; you must seek harmonious execution; you must complement each other's moves; and don't forget you will share the applause together."

That kind of counsel is very important and will deeply affect the beauty of the performance. But if that's all they know about the dance they're about to perform, they won't be able to do it. *They have to know the movements.* They have to know their different positions. They have to know who will fall and who will catch, who will run and who will stand. It is of the very essence of dance and drama that the players know the distinct movements they must make.

If they don't know their different assignments on the stage, there will be no drama, no dance.

2 CORINTHIANS 5:20–6:13

We are ambassadors for Christ, God making his appeal through us. We implore you on behalf of Christ, be reconciled to God. 21 For our sake he made him to be sin who knew no sin, so that in him we might become the righteousness of God. 1 Working together with him, then, we appeal to you not to receive the grace of God in vain. 2 For he says, "In a favorable time I listened to you, and in a day of salvation I have helped you." Behold, now is the favorable time; behold, now is the day of salvation. 3 We put no obstacle in anyone's way, so that no fault may be found with our ministry, 4 but as servants of God we commend ourselves in every way: by great endurance, in afflictions, hardships, calamities, 5 beatings, imprisonments, riots, labors, sleepless nights, hunger; 6 by purity, knowledge, patience, kindness, the Holy Spirit, genuine love; 7 by truthful speech, and the power of God; with the weapons of righteousness for the right hand and for the left; 8 through honor and dishonor, through slander and praise. We are treated as impostors, and yet are true; 9 as unknown, and yet well known; as dying, and behold, we live; as punished, and yet not killed; 10 as sorrowful, yet always rejoicing; as poor, yet making many rich; as having nothing, yet possessing everything. 11 We have spoken freely to you, Corinthians; our heart is wide open. 12 You are not restricted by us, but you are restricted in your own affections. 13 In return (I speak as to children) widen your hearts also.

10

Sorrowful Yet Always Rejoicing

The main point of this closing chapter is simple, powerful, and central. *What the world needs from the church is our indomitable joy in Jesus in the midst of suffering and sorrow.*

What the World Needs to See in Us

In my time at Bethlehem Baptist Church, I tried to lead in the experience of "sorrowful, yet always rejoicing." I address it again, now, as the tenth and final truth covered in this book—another wildly untamable, explosively uncontainable, and electrically future-creating reality; a truth that turns the world upside down.

It is because of this truth—"sorrowful, yet always rejoicing"—that I turn with dismay from church services that sound like talk radio—chipper, frisky, high-spirited chatter designed to make people feel lighthearted and playful and bouncy. I look at those services and say to myself, *Don't you know that people are sitting out there who are dying of cancer, whose marriage is a living hell, whose children have broken their hearts, who are barely making it financially, who have just lost their job, who are lonely and frightened and misunderstood and depressed? And you are going to try to create an atmosphere of bouncy, chipper, frisky, lighthearted, playful worship?*

Now some may read that and think, *Oh, so you imagine that what those people need is a morose, gloomy, sullen, dark, heavy atmosphere of solemnity?* But that's not my point. I'm saying that what those hurting people need is to see and feel indomitable joy in Jesus in the midst of suffering and sorrow. "Sorrowful, yet always rejoicing" (v. 10). They need to taste that these church people are not playing games. They are not using religion as a platform for the same old hyped-up self-help that the world offers every day. They need the greatness and the grandeur of God over their heads like galaxies of hope. They need the unfathomable crucified and risen Christ embracing them in love with blood all over his face and hands. And they need the thousand-mile-deep rock of God's word under their feet. They need to hear us sing with all our heart and soul,

> Ye fearful saints, fresh courage take;
> The clouds ye so much dread
> Are big with mercy and shall break
> In blessings on your head.
> His purposes will ripen fast,
> Unfolding every hour;
> The bud may have a bitter taste,
> But sweet will be the flower.

If you ask me, "Doesn't the unsaved world need to see Christians as happy in order to know the truth of our faith and be drawn to the great Savior?" My answer is, "Yes, yes, yes." *And* they need to see that our happiness is the indomitable work of Christ in the midst of our sorrow—a sorrow probably deeper than they have ever known, that we live with every day. They need to see "sorrowful, yet always rejoicing."

So let's put some of that rock under our feet now—the rock of God's word. Let's go to the Bible and see if these things are so.

Removing Obstacles and Commending the Ministry

Why have I put the emphasis on what the world needs? Why have I framed the main point of this chapter as, "What the world needs from the church is our indomitable joy in Jesus in the midst of suffering and sorrow?" The answer is in verses 3 and 4 of our text above. Paul says, "We put no obstacle in anyone's way, so that no fault may be found with our ministry, but as servants of God we commend ourselves in every way."

Paul is saying, "What I am about to do in this chapter is remove obstacles and commend our ministry—our life and message." He wants the church in Corinth, and the world, not to write him off, not to walk away, not to misunderstand who he is and what he teaches and whom he represents. He wants to win them.

It's amazing what he does here. Many savvy church-growth communicators today would have no categories for this method of removing obstacles and commending

Christianity. In fact, some might say Paul is not removing obstacles, but creating them. But that's not what's happening here; not at all.

Sufferings, Character, and Paradoxes

Let's watch Paul as he removes obstacles and commends his ministry. He does this in three ways.

Paul Describes the Sufferings He Endures for Christ

> We put no obstacle in anyone's way, so that no fault may be found with our ministry, but as servants of God we commend ourselves in every way: by great endurance, in afflictions, hardships, calamities, beatings, imprisonments, riots, labors, sleepless nights, hunger. (2 Corinthians 6:3–5)

How is this removing obstacles? How is this commending his ministry? Why is this not putting people off rather than drawing them in?" Hold that thought.

Paul Describes the Character He Tries to Show

> By purity, knowledge, patience, kindness, the Holy Spirit, genuine love; by truthful speech, and the power of God; with the weapons of righteousness for the right hand and for the left. (2 Corinthians 6:6–7)

Paul's reference to weapons is probably the sword of the Spirit in the right hand and the shield of faith in the left (Ephesians 6:16–17). So we see in these verses that Paul is not embittered or frustrated or angry or resentful due to all the afflictions and hardships and calamities and labors and sleepless nights. His spirit has not been broken by the pain of his ministry. Instead, by God's grace, he has shown patience and kindness and love. In the Holy Spirit, he has found resources to give and not to grumble; to be patient in God's timing rather than pity himself; to be kind to people rather than take it out on others.

Paul Describes the Paradoxes of the Christian Life

Through honor and dishonor, through slander and praise. We are treated as impostors, and yet are true; as unknown, and yet well known; as dying, and behold, we live; as punished, and yet not killed; as sorrowful, yet always rejoicing; as poor, yet making many rich; as having nothing, yet possessing every-thing. (2 Corinthians 6:8–10)

When you walk in the light, and minister in the power of Holy Spirit, and speak the truth in purity, knowledge, patience, kindness, and love (v. 6), some people will honor you and some will dishonor you (v. 8a); some will slander you, and some will praise you (v. 8b). And that dishonor and slander may come in the form of calling you an impostor (v. 8c). "You're not real. You're just a religious hypocrite."

Remember that Jesus said, "Woe to you, when all people speak well of you, for so their fathers did to the false prophets" (Luke 6:26). Which means that in Paul's mind a mixed reception (some honoring and praising, some dishonoring and slandering) was part of his commendation. It removed the obstacle that says, "You obviously can't be a true prophet, because all speak well of you."

Then come six more paradoxes. If you aren't careful, you might take these passages to mean that Paul is correcting false perceptions of Christians, but it's not quite like that. Every perception of the outsider he makes here has truth in it. But Paul is pointing out in each case that what is seen, although true, isn't the whole truth or even the main truth.

> You see us "as unknown, and yet [we are] well known" (v. 9a). *Yes, we are nobodies in the Roman empire, a tiny movement following a crucified and risen King. But oh, we are known by God, and that is what counts* (1 Corinthians 8:3; Galatians 4:9).

> You see us "as dying, and behold, we live" (v. 9b). *Yes, we die every day. We are crucified with Christ. Some of us are imprisoned and killed. But oh, we live because Christ is our life now, and he will raise us from the dead.*

> You see us "as punished, and yet [we are] not killed" (v. 9c). *Yes, we endure many human punishments and many divine chastenings, but over and over God has spared us from death. And he will spare us till our work is done.*

> You see us "as sorrowful, yet [we are] always rejoicing" (v. 10a). *Yes, we are sorrowful. There are countless reasons for our hearts to break. But in them all we do not cease to rejoice, and this is one of the greatest paradoxes of the Christian life!*

> You see us "as poor, yet [we are] making many rich" (v. 10b). *Yes, we are poor in this world's wealth. But we don't live to get rich on things, we live to make people rich on Jesus.*

> You see us "as having nothing, yet [we are] possessing everything" (v. 10c). *In one sense, we have*

*counted everything as loss for the surpassing worth of
knowing Christ Jesus* (Philippians 3:8). *But, in fact,
we are children of God, and if children, then heirs
of God and fellow heirs with Christ* (Romans 8:17).
In fact, to every Christian Paul says, "All things
are yours, whether Paul or Apollos or Cephas or
the world or life or death or the present or the
future—all are yours, and you are Christ's, and
Christ is God's" (1 Corinthians 3:21–23).

Removing the Principal Obstacle

Now step back and remember Paul's words in verse 3:
"We put no obstacle in anyone's way, so that no fault may
be found with our ministry, but as servants of God we
commend ourselves in every way." Then for seven verses he
removes obstacles to faith and commends the truth and
value of his ministry—his life, his message, his Lord. And
he does this in exactly the opposite way that the "prosperity gospel" does it.

What is the principal obstacle Paul removes? That
someone might think he is in the ministry for money, or
for earthly comfort and ease. He presents every evidence
he can think of to show that he is not a Christian—and
that he is not in the ministry—*because of* the worldly
benefits it can bring. There are many pastors today who
think just the opposite about this. They think that having a
lavish house and a lavish car and lavish clothes commends
their ministry. That's simply not the way Paul thought. He
thought that such things were obstacles.

Why? Because if they would entice anyone to Christ,
it would be for the wrong reason. It would be because they
think Jesus makes people rich, that he makes life com-

fortable and easy. No one should come to Christ for any
such reasons. Enticing people to Christ with prosperous
lifestyles or with chipper, bouncy, lighthearted, playful,
superficial banter, posing as joy in Christ, will attract some
people. But it will not do so by rightly displaying Christ
in his glory and rightly presenting the Christian life as the
Calvary Road. Many false conversions happen this way.

So Paul commends his ministry—his life, his message,
his Lord—by showing that *knowing* Christ, being known
by Christ, and having eternal life *with* Christ is better than
all earthly wealth and prosperity and comfort.

Two Pictures of "Sorrowful Yet Always Rejoicing"

We commend our life and ministry by afflictions. We
commend our life and ministry by calamities. We
commend our life and ministry by sleepless nights. What
does that mean? It means Christ is real to us, and Christ
is infinitely precious, more to be desired than any wealth
or comfort in this world. This is our commendation: *When
all around our soul gives way, he then is all our hope and stay.*
Here are two pictures of that in Scripture, although there
are many more.

Salt and Light

In the Sermon on the Mount, Jesus said, "Blessed are you
when others revile you and persecute you and utter all
kinds of evil against you falsely on my account. Rejoice
and be glad, for your reward is great in heaven" (Matthew
5:11–12). Do you think it is random that the next thing he

said was, "You are the salt of the earth… You are the light of the world?"

I don't think it was random. I think the tang of the salt that the world needs to taste, and the brightness of the light that the world needs to see, is precisely this indomitable joy in the midst of sorrow.

Joy in the midst of health? Joy in the midst of wealth and ease? And when everyone speaks well of you? Why would that mean anything to the world? The world has that already. But indomitable joy in the midst of sorrow—even when reviled and persecuted and spoken evil of—that the world does not have. The world cannot rejoice and be glad over these things. As Christians, we are often sorrowful, "sorrowful, *yet* always rejoicing." Joy in the midst of sorrow—this is exactly what Jesus came to give in this fallen, pain-filled, sin-wracked world. Paul's Kinsmen

Or consider Paul's experience of agony over the lostness of his Jewish kinsmen. Remember here that Paul himself wrote, "Rejoice in the Lord always; again I will say, rejoice" (Philippians 4:4). But he also wrote, "I have great sorrow and unceasing anguish in my heart. For I could wish that I myself were accursed and cut off from Christ for the sake of my brothers, my kinsmen according to the flesh" (Romans 9:2–3). Don't miss the terrible burden of that word *unceasing*. "I have great sorrow and unceasing anguish in my heart" because my kinsmen are perishing in unbelief, cut off from the Messiah.

Is Paul disobeying his own command to rejoice always? No. Because the experience of joy and the experience of sorrow are joined by the paradox of 2 Corinthians 6:10; we are "sorrowful, yet always rejoicing."

The World Needs This

Is this not what the world needs from us? Picture yourself at your favorite restaurant, sitting across a table from someone you care about very much, someone who is not a believer. You have shared the gospel before, and they have been unresponsive. God gives you the grace this time to plead with them. And he gives you the grace of tears. And you say, "I want so bad for you to believe and be a follower of Jesus with me. I want you to have eternal life. I want us to be with Christ forever together. I want you to share the joy of knowing that your sins are forgiven and that Jesus is your friend. And I can hardly bear the thought of losing you. It feels like a heavy stone in my chest."

Isn't that what the world needs from us? Not just an invitation to joy, not just a painful expression of concern, but the pain and the joy coming together in such a way that they have never seen anything like this. They have never been loved like this. They have never seen indomitable joy in Jesus in the midst of sorrow. And by God's grace, to them it may taste like the salt of the earth and look like the light of the world.

Indomitable joy in Jesus in the midst of suffering and sorrow—this was Paul's commendation of his ministry. May it be our commendation of Christ. It is no accident that Paul concluded the greatest chapter in the Bible—Romans 8—with words that are pointedly designed to sustain your joy and my joy in the face of suffering and loss.

> What then shall we say to these things? If God is for us, who can be against us? He who did not spare his own Son but gave him up for us all, how will he not also with him graciously give us all things? Who shall bring any charge against

God's elect? It is God who justifies. Who is to condemn? Christ Jesus is the one who died—more than that, who was raised—who is at the right hand of God, who indeed is interceding for us. Who shall separate us from the love of Christ? Shall tribulation, or distress, or persecution, or famine, or nakedness, or danger, or sword? As it is written, "For your sake we are being killed all the day long; we are regarded as sheep to be slaughtered." No, in [not instead of, but in!] all these things we are more than conquerors through him who loved us. For I am sure that neither death nor life, nor angels nor rulers, nor things present nor things to come, nor powers, nor height nor depth, nor anything else in all creation, will be able to separate us from the love of God in Christ Jesus our Lord (Romans 8:31–39).

So, Christian, let the world taste your indomitable joy in suffering and sorrow.

More about Joy Amidst Sorrow

SIX REASONS TO KEEP ON REJOICING NO MATTER WHAT

Beloved, do not be surprised at the fiery trial when it comes upon you to test you, as though something strange were happening to you. But rejoice insofar as you share Christ's sufferings, that you may also rejoice and be glad when his glory is revealed.
—1 Peter 4:12–13

We find here a command: "Rejoice insofar as you share Christ's sufferings." When you are thrown into the cellars of suffering, keep on rejoicing. When you are submerged in the sea of affliction, keep on rejoicing. In fact, keep on rejoicing not in spite of the affliction, but even because of it.

This is not a little life hack about the power of positive thinking. This is an utterly radical, abnormal, supernatural way to respond to suffering. It is not done in our own power or for our own honor. It is, rather, the way that spiritual exiles and aliens live on the earth for the glory of the Great King.

"Count it all joy, my brothers, when you meet trials of various kinds" (James 1:2) is foolish advice, except for one thing—God. In our passage above, Peter gives six reasons why we can keep on rejoicing when suffering comes. They all relate to God.

Keep on Rejoicing Because the Suffering Is Not an Accident, but a Plan

> Beloved, do not be surprised at the fiery trial when it comes upon you to test you, as though something strange were happening to you. (v. 12)

That trial isn't strange. It isn't absurd. It isn't meaningless. It is purposeful. It is for your testing. A few verses later Peter says, "Let those who *suffer according to God's will* entrust their souls to a faithful Creator" (1 Peter 4:19). Suffer… according to God's will. Suffering is not outside the will of God. It is in God's will. This is true even when Satan may be the immediate cause. God is sovereign over all things, including our suffering, and including Satan.

But why? For what purpose? Peter answers this in two ways. Suffering is "to test you" (v. 12), and then he says regarding suffering, "It is time for judgment to begin at the household of God; and if it begins with us, what will be the outcome for those who do not obey the gospel of God? And 'If the righteous is scarcely saved, what will become of the ungodly and the sinner?'" (v. 17–18). The point is that God's judgment is moving through the earth. The church does not escape, but the outcome is different for us. When the fire of judgment burns the church it is a testing, proving, purifying fire. When it burns the world, it either awakens or destroys.

Believers pass through the testing fire of God's judgment—not because he hates us, but because he loves us and wills our purity. God hates sin so much and loves his children so much that he will spare us no pain to rid us of what he hates.

So the first reason Peter gives for why we can keep on rejoicing when suffering comes is that suffering is not accidental; it is planned. It is a testing. It is purifying fire. It proves and strengthens real faith, and it consumes "performance faith."

Alexander Solzhenitsyn had long been impressed with the patience and longsuffering of Russian believers. One night in prison in Siberia, Boris Kornfeld, a Jewish doctor, sat up with Solzhenitsyn and told him the story of his conversion to Christ. That same night, Kornfeld was clubbed to death. Solzhenitsyn said that Kornfeld's last words were, "lay upon me as an inheritance . . . It was only when I lay there on rotting prison straw that I sensed within myself the first stirrings of good... Bless you, prison, for having been my life."

We can have strong hope that the sufferings of our own day will bring purity and life to many, and awaken many. Suffering is not accidental; it is purposeful.

Keep on Rejoicing Because Your Suffering as a Christian Is an Evidence of Your Union with Christ

> *But rejoice insofar as you share Christ's sufferings.*
> (v. 13)

In other words, your sufferings are not merely your own. They are also Christ's. This is cause for rejoicing because it means you are united to Christ. Joseph Tson, a Romanian pastor who stood up to Ceausescu's repressions of Christianity, wrote,

> This union with Christ is the most beautiful subject in the Christian life. It means that I am not a lone fighter here: I am an extension of Jesus Christ. When I was beaten in Romania, he suffered in my body. It is not my suffering: I only had the honor to share his sufferings. (undated paper, "A Theology of Martyrdom")

Keep on rejoicing, because your sufferings as a Christian are not merely yours, but Christ's, and they give evidence of your union with him.

Keep on Rejoicing Because This Joy Will Strengthen Your Assurance That When Christ Comes in Glory, You Will Rejoice Forever with Him

> *But rejoice insofar as you share Christ's sufferings,*
> *that you may also rejoice and be glad when his glory*
> *is revealed.* (v. 13)

The idea is that we are to keep on rejoicing now, so that we may also rejoice then. Our joy now, through suffering, *is a means of attaining our joy then*, a thousand-fold in glory.

First there is suffering, then there is glory. Peter said

that the spirit "predicted the sufferings of Christ and the subsequent glories" (1 Peter 1:11; cf. 5:1). And Paul said that if we "suffer with him" we will "be glorified with him" (Romans 8:17). First the suffering, and then the glory— both for Jesus and for those who are united to him.

If we become embittered at life and the pain it deals us, we are not preparing to rejoice at the revelation of Christ's glory. Keep on rejoicing now in suffering, in order that you might rejoice with exultation at the revelation of his glory.

Keep on Rejoicing in Suffering Because Then the Spirit of Glory and of God Rests upon You

> *If you are insulted for the name of Christ, you are blessed, because the Spirit of glory and of God rests upon you.* (v. 14)

This means that in the hour of greatest trial, there is a great consolation. In great suffering on earth there is great support from heaven. You may think now that you will not be able to bear it. But if you are Christ's, you will be able to bear it, because he will come to you and rest upon you. As Rutherford said, the Great King keeps his finest wine in the cellar of affliction. He does not bring it out to serve with chips on sunny afternoons. He keeps it for extremities.

And what is this? What is the Spirit of glory and of God resting on you in suffering? The answer is simply that you will find out when you need it. The Spirit will reveal enough of glory and enough of God to satisfy your soul and carry you through.

Seek to be holy; seek to bring truth; seek to bear witness; and do not turn aside from risk. And sooner or

later you will experience the Spirit of glory and of God
resting upon you in suffering.

Keep on Rejoicing in Suffering Because This Glorifies God
> If anyone suffers as a Christian, let him not be
> ashamed, but let him glorify God in that name
> (v. 16)

Glorifying God means showing by your actions and
attitudes that God is glorious to you—that he is valuable, precious, desirable, satisfying. And the greatest way
to show that someone satisfies your heart is to keep on
rejoicing in that person when all other supports for your
satisfaction are falling away. When you keep rejoicing in
God in the midst of suffering, it shows that God, and not
other things, is the great source of your joy.

Paul Brand, the missionary surgeon to India, tells the
story of his mother, a missionary in India whose life sym-
bolized devotion to the glory of God through suffering.

> For Mother, pain was a frequent companion, as
> was sacrifice. I say it kindly and in love, but in
> old age, Mother had little of physical beauty left
> in her. The rugged conditions, combined with
> the crippling falls and her battles with typhoid,
> dysentery, and malaria, had made her a thin,
> hunched-over old woman. Years of exposure to
> wind and sun had toughened her facial skin into
> leather and furrowed it with wrinkles as deep and
> extensive as any I have seen on a human face…
> Mother knew that as well as anyone—for the last
> 20 years of her life she refused to keep a mirror in
> her house (*Christianity Today*, January 10, 1994, 23).

Twenty years of ministry without a mirror. Do you get it? *She* was the mirror. And God was the light and the glory.

Keep on Rejoicing in Suffering Because Your Creator Is Faithful to Care for Your Soul

> *Therefore let those who suffer according to God's will entrust their souls to a faithful Creator while doing good.* (v. 19)

Degrees of suffering and forms of affliction will differ for each of us. But this one thing we will all have in common until Jesus comes: we will all die. We will come to that awesome moment of reckoning. If you have time to ponder and reflect, you may see your whole life played out before you as you weigh whether it has been well spent. You will tremble at the unspeakable reality that soon you will face God. And the destiny of your soul will be irrevocable.

Will you rejoice in that hour? You will if you entrust your soul to a faithful Creator. He created your soul for his glory. He is faithful to that glory and to all who love it and live for it. Now is the time to show where your treasure is—in heaven or on earth. Now is the time to shine with the glory of God. Trust him. And keep on rejoicing.

✻ desiringGod

Everyone wants to be happy. Our website was born
and built for happiness. We want people everywhere
to understand and embrace the truth that God is most
glorified in us when we are most satisfied in him. We've
collected more than thirty years of John Piper's speaking
and writing, including translations into more than forty
languages. We also provide a daily stream of new written,
audio, and video resources to help you find truth, purpose,
and satisfaction that never end. And it's all available free
of charge, thanks to the generosity of people who've been
blessed by the ministry.

If you want more resources for true happiness, or if
you want to learn more about our work at Desiring God,
we invite you to visit us at www.desiringGod.org.

———————————————

www.desiringGod.org

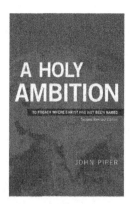

A Holy Ambition
To Preach Where Christ Has Not Been Named

John Piper | 200 pages

The definitive collection of John Piper's missions-oriented sermons, drawn from his more than 35 years of ministry.

bit.ly/holyambition

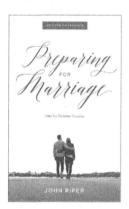

Preparing for Marriage
Help for Christian Couples

John Piper | 86 pages

As you prepare for marriage, dare to dream with God.

bit.ly/prep-for-marriage

The Joy Project:
An Introduction to Calvinism

(with Study Guide)

Tony Reinke
Foreword by John Piper | 168 pages

True happiness isn't found. It finds you.

bit.ly/JOYPROJECT

Don't miss these fully inductive Bible studies for women from Keri Folmar!

Loved by churches. Endorsed by Kristi Anyabwile, Connie Dever, Gloria Furman, Kathleen Nielson, and Diane Schreiner.

*Six volumes and growing! **Visit bit.ly/DITWStudies***

10 weeks   *10 weeks*   *10 weeks*

Joy! (Philippians)   *Faith* (James)   *Grace* (Ephesians)

11 weeks   *11 weeks*   *9 weeks*

Son of God (Gospel of Mark, 2 volumes)   *Zeal* (Titus)

Do More Better
A Practical Guide to Productivity

Tim Challies | 114 pages

Don't try to do it all. Do more good. Better.

bit.ly/domorebetter

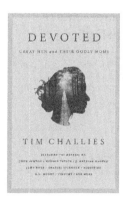

Devoted
Great Men and Their Godly Moms

Tim Challies | 128 pages

Women shaped the men who changed the world.

bit.ly/devotedbook

Run to Win
The Lifelong Pursuits of a Godly Man

Tim Challies | 163 pages

Plan to run, train to run…run to win.

bit.ly/RUN2WIN

Who Am I?
Identity in Christ

Jerry Bridges | 91 pages

Jerry Bridges unpacks Scripture to give the Christian eight clear, simple, interlocking answers to one of the most essential questions of life.

bit.ly/WHOAMI

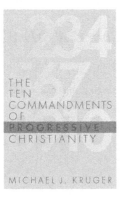

The Ten Commandments of Progressive Christianity

Michael J. Kruger | 56 pages

A cautionary look at ten dangerously appealing half-truths.

bit.ly/TENCOM

Endorsed by Collin Hansen, Kevin DeYoung, Michael Horton

Grieving, Hope and Solace
When a Loved One Dies in Christ

Albert N. Martin | 112 pages

*There is comfort for the grief.
There are answers to the questions.*

bit.ly/GriefHope